S0-ARL-380

There are some people who are so good at talking the talk. But Charla, she walks the walk. She trusts the Lord with all her heart, even when that looks like the hardest way. How can harder be better? Well, I guess harder to the flesh is better for the spirit. Trust isn't natural; it's supernatural. And, it is the way to the blessing of God! "Lord Almighty, blessed is the man who TRUSTS in you" (Psalm 84:12, NIV). Charla is just the insightful, patient, Spirit-led person to guide you on the journey of trust. Enjoy, life gets better from here.

—*Nicole Crank*
Co-founder and Co-Lead Pastor, Faith Church
Author, Hi God: It's Me Again and Goal Getters

A small measure of relational trust, when held carefully, can grow into a lifelong shade of openness and safety. Through the well-lived days of Charla, her experience comes from a rich place in life full of deep faith in her Lord and her relationships with people. May the words held in your hands give you the wisdom to be a gracious, consistent friend to those around you and the tools to develop the potential friendships you have currently. Let it test the spirit of every relationship you have to cause you to walk together in greater peace and unity.

—*Dianna Nepstad*
Pastor, Fellowship Church, Antioch, California

TrustWorthy will touch your heart and challenge you to grow deeper in your relationships. Since trust is so important in our personal and working relationships, this book is a must-read. Charla gives great insight through her own personal journey and transparency. She will help you let go, believe again, and move forward. Your ability to trust is vital. Trust is hard to define, but we know when it's lost. Whether you are a leader, coach, parent, teacher, or friend, *TrustWorthy* is fundamental for the success of your relationships.

—*Sheila Craft*
Co-Pastor, Elevate Life Cathedral, Frisco, Texas

Trust is sacred in every relationship. All meaningful relationships are built on trust. Healthy relationships bring joy, but, when we entrust our heart to the wrong person, it can be devastating, gut-wrenching, and extremely painful. Many of us, betrayed by a boyfriend, spouse, family member, or friend, have had our hearts shattered and our self-esteem destroyed. Stunned, we wonder how we did not see that, and sadly we end up carrying that painful experience into all our future relationships not knowing whom to trust.

What if we knew how to prevent this heartache? What if we knew how to spot signs of unhealthiness before we jumped into the relationship? What if we knew who is safe to trust and who is not?

In this book, *TrustWorthy: Deepening the Relationships You Want and Avoiding the Ones You Don't,* Charla Turner opens up about her own heartache. Who better than she is able to give us the necessary tools needed to heal, so we don't have to walk around wounded for the rest of our lives. Charla also teaches us how to spot those unhealthy signs beforehand, so we can avoid unnecessary drama, knowing whom to trust and whom not to so that we can enjoy great satisfying relationships in our lives.

—*Maria Durso*
Overseer, Saints Church
Author and Conference Speaker

In *Trustworthy: Deepening the Relationships You Want and Avoiding the Ones You Don't,* Charla does a masterful job handling one of the foundational components of healthy relationships—trust. Without it, there is no genuine relationship. This book provides wonderful insight concerning trust and its importance. It also pinpoints great "signs" to look for that will help guide you in your relationships—present and future. It's a must-read!

—*Dr. Nina Bronner*
Minister of Worship and the Arts
Word of Faith Family Worship Cathedral

We have all felt the sting of betrayal and broken trust. Charla meets us in the midst of those wounds, and through her life experiences, walks us through a journey towards healing. She provides valuable wisdom in determining whom to trust, how to keep your heart safe, and how to trust again after experiencing betrayal. *TrustWorthy* is for everyone who wants to develop and deepen healthy, safe relationships.

—*Grace Klein*
Focus 412

Life is filled with relationships. They can become wonderful opportunities to grow, or they can be filled with all kinds of obstacles leaving one depleted and defeated. Trust is a vital key to unlocking true relational potential filling life with great joy. If you are weary of broken trust, this book is for you. Between these pages, you will discover the power of trust, how to build and maintain trust, as well as how to guard and protect it. Charla is a brilliant communicator who understands the power of trust when it is valued correctly. This book will revolutionize your paradigm and ignite necessary changes for a lifetime of trust.

—*Jillian Chambers*

Charla Turner's tender words strengthen me every time I'm with her. When she ministers, hearts instantly open up and are transformed. This book is an incredible reflection of Charla's heart to restore people's lives with beautiful transparency and incredible wisdom. I can't wait to share it with others!

—*LaCinda Bloomfield*
Speaklove Women

Charla is easily one of my "go-to" friends; she is Word wealthy and loves Jesus with her whole heart! Her passion for personal growth is seemingly insatiable, and the insights in *TrustWorthy* reflect that. Charla shares from a place of vulnerability that ministered healing to my heart at a deep level. She is inspiring, intentional, and full of wisdom and discernment as read in the pages of this book! I encourage everyone to read *TrustWorthy* today!

—*Holly Anderson*
Co-Pastor, Living Word Bible Church, Mesa, Arizona

Oh, how I wish there were an instruction manual on trust! Wait a minute, there is. *TrustWorthy*, while it may not be an instruction manual, is definitely a book filled with wisdom and insight about this deceptively complicated little word—trust. Through personal trials and years of living it out, Charla shines a light on how to overcome the tough situations we all face throughout our lives. Sometimes, when trust has been broken, it's hard to trust again. Get back on track with *TrustWorthy*.

—*Tabatha Claytor*
Co-Pastor, Alive Church

TRUST *Worthy*

How to deepen the relationships you need and avoid the ones you don't.

CHARLA TURNER

AVAIL

Copyright © 2022 by Charla Turner

Published by AVAIL

All rights reserved. No portion of this book may be reproduced, stored in a retrieval system, or transmitted in any form or by any means—electronic, mechanical, photocopy, recording, scanning, or other—except for brief quotations in critical reviews or articles, without prior written permission of the author.

Scripture quotations marked KJV are taken from the King James Version of the Bible. Public domain. | Scripture quotations marked NIV are taken from the Holy Bible, New International Version®, NIV®. Copyright © 1973, 1978, 1984, 2011 by Biblica, Inc.™ Used by permission of Zondervan. All rights reserved worldwide. www.zondervan.com. The "NIV" and "New International Version" are trademarks registered in the United States Patent and Trademark Office by Biblica, Inc.™ | Scripture quotations marked NKJV are taken from the New King James Version®. Copyright © 1982 by Thomas Nelson. Used by permission. All rights reserved. | Scripture quotations marked NLT are taken from the Holy Bible, New Living Translation, copyright © 1996, 2004, 2015 by Tyndale House Foundation. Used by permission of Tyndale House Publishers, Inc., Carol Stream, Illinois 60188. All rights reserved. | Scripture quotations marked MSG are taken from THE MESSAGE, copyright © 1993, 1994, 1995, 1996, 2000, 2001, 2002 by Eugene H. Peterson. Used by permission of NavPress. All rights reserved. Represented by Tyndale House Publishers, Inc. | Scripture quotations marked ESV are from The ESV® Bible (The Holy Bible, English Standard Version®), copyright © 2001 by Crossway, a publishing ministry of Good News Publishers. Used by permission. All rights reserved. | Scripture quotations marked TPT are from The Passion Translation®. Copyright © 2017, 2018 by Passion & Fire Ministries, Inc. Used by permission. All rights reserved. ThePassionTranslation.com. | Scripture quotations marked NASB have been taken from the (NASB®) New American Standard Bible®, Copyright © 2020 by The Lockman Foundation. Used by permission. All rights reserved. www.lockman.org | Scripture quotations marked BSB are from The Holy Bible, Berean Study Bible, BSB, Copyright ©2016, 2020 by Bible Hub Used by Permission. All Rights Reserved Worldwide. | Scripture quotations marked TLV are taken from the Holy Scriptures, Tree of Life Version*. Copyright © 2014, 2016 by the Tree of Life Bible Society. Used by permission of the Tree of Life Bible Society.

For foreign and subsidiary rights, contact the author.

Cover design: Sara Young

Cover Photo: Andrew van Tilborgh

ISBN: 978-1-957369-38-9   1 2 3 4 5 6 7 8 9 10

Printed in the United States of America

I dedicate this book to my children.

To my first baby in heaven:

I never gave you a chance at life on earth, and that decision is one I will regret for the rest of my life. Although I know I am forgiven by God, it took me a long time to forgive myself. My hope is that I will hold you one day in heaven where no more pain can ever touch either one of us.

To my second baby in heaven:

I loved you before I knew a single thing about you. Miscarriage and abortion are so different, yet the ache and grief of what could have been are both deeply painful. Know that you were created in love. Your dad and I missed knowing the gift of you, but we are excited to meet you in heaven one day.

To my heaven on earth children—Micha, Presley, and Madelyn:

I am so grateful that God allowed me to experience the gift of motherhood. You have changed my life in all the best ways. Raising you exposed all my weaknesses and caused me to change for the better. You have taught me what unconditional love feels like. You three are my greatest trust exercise. You are all filled with greatness, and I love you endlessly. You make me so proud, and I hope I make you proud too.

CONTENTS

Foreword

This book, *TrustWorthy*, needs to be added to your library. It's almost as important to read as your Bible. It's full of life-giving, heart-healing truth bombs that immediately heal the deepest secrets of your heart. While reading *TrustWorthy*, I found myself—literally—releasing things from my heart that I hadn't even known I was holding onto. Chapter by chapter, Charla Turner paints a revelatory picture of how to discern and connect to truth about trust. It's transforming the wisdom on this topic that she unfolds so beautifully.

Let's just be honest; trusting is not easy. It's one of the areas in which the enemy fights us because trusting is necessary in every healthy relationship. The day you were born, the journey began. It started with you trusting your parents. Sometimes they fail us. Sometimes they are broken also by someone they trusted, and the cycle begins. The generational curse starts. If it wasn't your parents, it was the bully on the playground that you trusted to be your friend but who betrayed you. Maybe your spouse, whom you trusted to keep their vows, betrayed you. Maybe a best friend with whom you trusted your secrets used them against you. Whatever the circumstances, the enemy was able to manipulate your heart and break you.

This amazing book will help you heal and allow you to encounter the wisdom you need to conquer your life and live it to the fullest without being afraid to trust the people that God has sent to you. Trusting others in friendship, romance, business, government, and church is an art that is much like a dance. Timing, preparation, ability, strength, style, vulnerability, and risk are essential. After reading *TrustWorthy*, you will soar in these areas.

I pray that God blows your mind as He turns your scars into stars and your pain into your pulpit, while you are being filled with God's love, so you can be the world changer you were created to be.

Happy healing, and happy growing to you! I love you.

—Kim Jones aka Real Talk Kim
Author and Pastor, Limitless Church
www.realtalkkim.com

Preface

Dear Friend,

My hope is that you will find healing and hope in this book. I share some of my own stories of betrayal because I want you to know that you are not alone. It is possible to heal from the pain of past betrayal and have healthy relationships in your future. I hope you find useful tools inside the pages that will help you navigate relationships in such a way that you feel confident and secure in them.

We are all on this journey of finding, deepening, and discerning the relationships we most need and avoiding unnecessary pain. There is a quote by Haruki Murakami: "Pain is inevitable, but suffering is optional." My hope is to help you eliminate some of the unnecessary pain in relationships as it relates to trust. May your heart be healed and free from painful past hurts, and may your future be filled with deep connections and greater intimacy.

Acknowledgments

My wonderful husband, Michael: Thank you for taking me on that first blind date, being gentle with my guarded heart, introducing me to a deeper relationship with God, believing in me, loving me, and building a beautiful family with me. Next to Jesus, you are the best thing that's ever happened to me. I adore you. I love you, and I want to spend the rest of my life making you glad you chose me.

Dr. Samuel Chand: Thank you for being a global leader who, in spite of leading millions of people, always sees the "one." Thank you for believing in us.

Debbie Chand: Thank you for making this process smooth and excellent. You are a joy to talk to. Your voice is filled with kindness, and your sense of humor is the best!

Hannah Zello: Thank you for helping me organize my thoughts and communicate my story. Thank you for using your gifts to help others and reflect God's love for them.

Rob and Melissa Jones: You are truly our best friends and deepest confidants. Thank you for showing us trust in motion for over twenty-five years. Your friendship means the world to us.

Milan Ford: Thank you for sharing your wisdom always but especially through some painful seasons. Thank you for believing in me. You will never know how much that has meant. Everyone should be so blessed to have someone like you in their life. You make everyone around you better.

TPC Staff: You are an answer to our prayers. Thank you for your honor, integrity, and love. The culture we have now is better than I could have ever imagined. I cherish you.

Sheila Craft: Thank you for being a loving mentor, a wise source of advice, and a true example of a godly woman in every way. I trust you, and I love you.

Nicole Crank: Thank you for believing in me. Your impact on my life is undeniable. Your deposits of faith, courage, wisdom, hope, and trust will forever be a part of me. Thank you for the relationship gifts I have found in our roundtable. They are of immeasurable worth. I love you.

Introduction:

WHEN TRUST GOES WRONG

The best way to find out if you can trust somebody is to trust them.
—Ernest Hemingway

"Let Go Of The Stone"[1]
"Let go of the stone if you don't want to drown
In the sea of heartache that's draggin' you down
It's pulling you under and you keep hangin' on
If I'm ever gonna save you—let go of the stone...."

I t's been over thirty years, but I still remember this old country song playing through the radio as I drove to see my counselor. As I passed through a few traffic lights, I realized it wasn't just John Anderson who was singing but God who was trying to speak to me through the song.

It was a day I will never forget. I was lying flat-faced on the chocolate brown shag carpet of my counselor's office in what later became an ocean full of tears the more I shared. A six-year-long relationship with the man I had trusted, given my whole heart to, and believed one day I would spend the rest of my life with was now suddenly all over. It felt as though my entire life had been shattered.

My trust had been broken. And my body, as a result of this relationship, had been broken too. The guilt and shame of what I had done were eating away at my heart and making my soul ache with

---

1   John Anderson, vocalist, "Let Go Of The Stone," by Max D. Barnes and Max T. Barnes, released February 11, 1992, track 4 on *Seminole Wind*, BNA Records.

pain. I never thought in a million years that I would be capable of participating in such an act. But I did.

After sharing with my counselor what had happened, he graciously left the room and gave me some time to talk alone with God. I'm not sure how long he left me in there, but it was long enough to unlock every emotion I had locked away and begin placing a name to every tear that was coming down my face.

The slow-falling tears I chose to name "deep regret."

The ones that only fell when I blinked my eyes I named "scorning shame" and "stinging rejection."

Yet there were others that crawled all the way down to my chin that I named "a hatred of myself."

When my counselor returned to the room, it dawned on me that I had confessed my deepest, darkest secret to someone who had been just a "stranger" to me a few hours before. His name was Kris Ramsahai, an Indian missionary, who, using the most calming voice and beautiful dialect, said four short words to me that were full of the kindness and mercy of God.

"Jesus still loves you."

When he said it, I immediately had an inner assurance that what he was speaking came straight from the heart of God. I fully believed and trusted that what he had spoken was full of faith and did not have a shred of unbelief attached to it, despite what I had done, perhaps because it was void of shame.

But he didn't stop there.

"There is nothing you can do to make God love you any less or any more ... but, you must forgive yourself, forgive your boyfriend, and then let him go."

Kris had no idea how many times I had thoughts about letting him go, wondering whether or not he was the person I was supposed to be with. Kris had no idea how many nights—as I endured years of verbal abuse—I had prayed to God asking for Him to change my boyfriend into the man I wanted and needed him to be. At the young age of twenty-one, I had given my full trust to someone I never should have, and now I was paying the consequences. Why couldn't I just let this stone go? What do you do when trust goes wrong?

I wish I could say that was the last time I misplaced my trust, but it wasn't. I have done so with family and friends, in business, and even within the local church I help serve and lead. Whenever trust is misplaced and goes wrong, it leaves you shocked, saddened, wounded, and in a state of hopelessness. If polled, ten out of ten people would probably say that they have had the precious gift of trust betrayed at least once. Because trust is essential to our marriages, our parenting, our workplaces, and the decisions we make almost every day, when it is betrayed, it can darken the lens through which we see our lives.

I am still amazed that I needed my counselor that day to confirm something I already knew, but sometimes, that's what we need: a confirmation. We need people in our lives to help us learn *how* to trust, *whom* to trust, *when* to trust, and how to heal and trust *again*. If you are struggling with trust, I want you to know that you are not alone. As I sit here now, at the age of fifty-one, I am still discovering what trust is and what it is not. I'm doing all I can to remain in a posture of growth where I can become trustworthy and ensure that the relationships I have around me now are trustworthy as well.

Living a life of trust requires intentionality, and I am excited to journey along with you through this book to help you do what is needed to fully embrace the value that trust must have in your life. I love what the classic American novelist Ernest Hemingway once wrote: "The best way to find out if you can trust somebody is to trust them."

Thank you for trusting me. I look forward to you discovering how to trust (again).

Chapter 1

THE ORIGIN OF TRUST ISSUES: WHERE DID IT ALL GO WRONG?

In every end, there is also a beginning.
—Libba Bray, *A Great and Terrible Beauty*

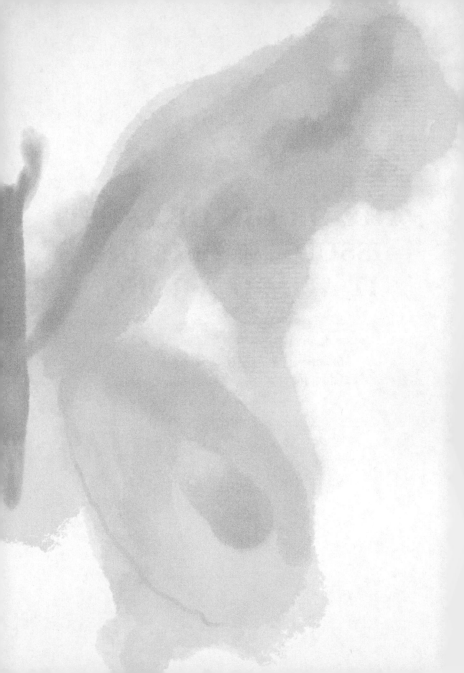

Whenever you and I give another person our trust, it can feel as though we are handing them a piece of our heart. We all know people who are quick to trust others with no reservations. However, for most of us, trusting someone wholeheartedly does not come easy. We tend to hold suspicion close and cynicism closer, particularly because of what we experienced in our past relationships, even those we grew up with in our homes. If we'd had trustworthy caregivers early on as children and our needs met in a consistent environment, where we felt safe and secure, then perhaps we would be more trusting. But if our foundation were faulty, trusting others becomes more challenging.

Whether it was through some form of betrayal, abuse, neglect, or hardship, we have all been let down by people in our life. We can blame it on unmet expectations or a simple misunderstanding, but none of us is without some degree of trust issues. As a woman who has been in ministry for over twenty years, I can't count—because there have been so many—the number of discussions I have had with people about whom they could or could not trust because of something that a person did in the past. The truth is that each of us has a set of lenses that we see others through. It has been shaped by our past personal experiences. It's quite common for us to rely entirely too much on the rearview window of our life, seeing what's ahead of us based on what may have happened behind us. And just in case you feel as though you're the only one, let's take a look at some examples in the Bible that would tell you otherwise.

In the very first book of the Bible, the book of Genesis, we see a trust issue emerge between Adam, Eve, and God. It's amazing to know that at humanity's very beginning, trust was an issue. In fact, the story of Adam and Eve is ALL about trust—a trust that was not only tested, but it was also broken. Adam and Eve's broken trust in God and their decision to choose the created things over the Creator not only impacted them, they also impacted everyone who came after them. Their decision to choose the voice of a serpent (a created thing) over trusting God, the One who formed and created all of life, was the poorest decision they could have ever made. The voice of the One who nurtured them and walked with them was denied their full trust and exchanged for the deceitful voice of the enemy. Despite being placed inside a perfect garden and granted dominion over everything in it, they were manipulated by the seeds of doubt this serpent sowed into their hearts.

Perhaps you're saying to yourself, *Well, that would never have happened to me!* Maybe you think you would be strong enough to avoid that serpent and maintain your trust in God. However, if we're honest with ourselves, all of us have had an Adam-and-Eve type of experience before. The more self-aware we become, the more we can empathize with Eve and the severe case of FOMO (aka fear of missing out) that she obviously was experiencing. Safely looking at Adam and Eve from the outside in, perhaps we think we could have just shouted, "Don't trust that snake!" and that would have been the end of it. But just as it did for Eve, it will prove true for many of us: when we get disconnected from the goodness of God, we will become connected to the lies that the enemy wants us to believe.

When we get disconnected from the goodness of God, we will become connected to the lies that the enemy wants us to believe.

I love this quote from Ignatius of Loyola: "Sin is the unwillingness to trust that what God wants for me is only my deepest happiness." It often seems that it's just too good to be true that God would desire our deepest happiness, but it's true. Despite our unmet desires and unanswered questions about the goodness of God, He wants what is best for us. Friends, that is what the gospel is all about!

Our deepest happiness is found when we receive the mercy and grace of God and enter into a relationship with the One who loves us most. It's a great adventure. Sometimes, there is conflict in our minds between happiness and holiness. If we could ever marry those two thoughts, I think we might find true satisfaction. Instead, we often find the two ideas oppositional. Likewise, Ignatius, who spoke of God wanting our deepest happiness, is also quoted as saying, "True, I am in love with suffering, but I do not know if I deserve the honor."

Could true happiness be found in both suffering and pleasure? Perhaps. Is it possible that our deepest happiness is actually found in it all—suffering, pleasure, and holiness—but we just can't seem to trust God enough all the way through the process?

We have all tried one way or another to take our share of shortcuts. We've gotten caught in what feels good, and it is that selfish desire that drowns out the voice of our God. The enemy is very crafty as he entices us and calls out to the desire within us. He puts thoughts in our mind so often that, over time, we believe they're our own. Whenever our temptations and desires connect, they can crowd out the truth. Trust goes wrong when we believe the thoughts of the created over the Creator.

Trust goes wrong when we believe the thoughts
of the created over the Creator.

....

The truth is that we can always trust God. Babbie Mason said it best in the chorus of "Trust His Heart," a song she cowrote with Eddie Carswell and performed: "God is too good to be unkind, and He is too wise to be mistaken. And when we cannot trace His hand, we must trust His heart."[2] When we see how the heart of God is bent towards us, specifically through the price He paid on the cross, we can rest assured that we can always place our trust in God. To know that He laid down His life and suffered a brutal death just so we could be forgiven is the greatest victory you and I will ever know. Our God won victory over death, hell, and the grave, and our eternity can now be spent with Him. All that is required of us is to confess that He is Lord and believe in His goodness. And that belief—that He is who He says He is—is deeply rooted in trust.

Since we see that the origin of misplaced trust was found at the beginning of humanity in the garden of Eden, we have to understand the origin of our trust must start with trusting God, then ourselves. We can only trust well when we start by trusting God. There will be times when we have to go to the beginning of our own relationships to find the origin of when trust went wrong with us. When we go back to our most painful moments, we realize that we placed our trust in someone who was not trustworthy. Going back helps us find clues and trust patterns that eventually led to some painful betrayals. Maybe we ignored the obvious red flags and wrote them off with excuses because we so wanted the relationship to work out, or maybe we were deceived by people who were deceived themselves into believing a lie perpetrated by the enemy.

---

2   Babbie Mason, vocalist, "Trust His Heart," by Babbie Mason and Eddie Carswell, released February 28, 2006, track 14 on *All the Best*, Spring Hill Music Group.

The Bible is full of stories of betrayal and broken trust, each having a different starting and ending point. Some of these stories are too painful to even read, because, when I read them, I tend to imagine what those in each story must have felt when those closest to them violated their trust so deeply. Let's take the story of Amnon and Tamar, for example.

The story of Amnon and Tamar is one of a family betrayal of epic proportions. Tamar was the stepdaughter of King David, and she had two brothers: one named Absalom who was said to be very handsome, and a half-brother named Amnon. Her half-brother Amnon became obsessed with her beauty and was overtaken by his lust for her. He did not display any real affection or care for her evidenced by the fact that he took her virginity from her by tricking her. He lured her to his quarters under the false premise that he was sick. Once she arrived, he raped her. Her very own brother, the one she came to help in his moment of weakness, took advantage of Tamar. His hate for her was that strong.

I found it interesting that leading up to this moment, Amnon had an opportunity to do something about his obsession with his sister. When he first became obsessed with her, he consulted with his cousin on the best way to take advantage of her. I wonder what could have happened if he had just asked a God-honoring person for advice about this? Someone who would have told him this was wrong. Someone who would have provided some accountability and truth. I'm quite sure a lot would have been different. I can only imagine the private comments he was making about Tamar or any other behavior he was demonstrating towards her! Had that happened around a person of integrity and godly character, surely that would have been an immediate warning sign to speak up and say something. But no one around Amnon addressed it. No one. Once the act was done, even King David, who the Bible says was angry, took no action against Amnon, which made matters worse.

What pain Tamar must have experienced that day! The shame and shock of someone within her own family doing such a heinous act, only to discover no one would step up and do something about it, breaks my heart. Tamar was not only left with a broken body but with a broken heart as well. Her other brother, Absalom, who had little shame in demonstrating his anger, sought to get revenge against Amnon for what he did by luring him to a feast. Absalom invited all of his brothers to the feast as well. Once Amnon was full of food and wine, Absalom's servants killed him. Weak from indulging all night long, Amnon was murdered at his own brother's orders. Just as he had violated his sister, his brother violated him. He clearly reaped what he sowed.

It reminds me of the biblical story of Esther. There are a few similarities. Haman plotted to have Esther's cousin Mordecai and the Jewish people wiped out, yet, in the end, what Haman plotted as a cruel death for another is what happened to him. Proverbs 6:12-15 (ESV) warns:

A worthless person, a wicked man, goes about with crooked speech, winks with his eyes, signals with his feet, points with his finger, with perverted heart devises evil, continually sowing discord; therefore calamity will come upon him suddenly; in a moment he will be broken beyond healing.

This scripture certainly was true for both Amnon and Haman.

Betrayal was all around King David's family and left a wake of destruction. His entire family and everyone around them were affected. Absalom went on to, ironically, sleep with David's concubine, thereby betraying David and attempting to usurp his authority. The cycle continued down the family line. Each person simply took what they wanted rather than honor and follow God. The array of emotions and pain that was inflicted was immense.

We are, perhaps, the most familiar with the story of Joseph who was betrayed by his brothers because of their envy. The favor that Joseph had with their father was symbolized by the coat Joseph was given. This caused his brothers to have negative emotions that led them to want to erase Joseph from the family. A dream that Joseph shared—in which he would be the leader over them—furthered their desires to get rid of him. What was the origin of this thought process? One brother coming into agreement with the enemy is all it took to get this betrayal started. One brother may have begun to give voice to the envious and prideful feelings he had. Maybe another came into agreement. Maybe it was the brother with the most influence among the others who started it all. Maybe this caused the murmuring to spread until they devised an action to carry out the betrayal.

What must Joseph have felt when he was in that pit? The people he loved most and thought would be happy for his success hated him so much that they wanted him gone. He must have felt such deep agony. He deeply loved his family, yet they wanted him either dead or far away from them. Of course, we know there was great redemption and reconciliation at the end of the story where love and forgiveness flowed, but in that pit, the pain was real.

In fact, I believe we can learn much from the life of Joseph and especially his response when His brothers returned. He wept. He demonstrated genuine love for them. He forgave them and blessed them. He gave them provisions, and he broke the cycle. That beautiful act of forgiveness and generosity no doubt changed the family legacy forever. His brothers probably told that story to their children and grandchildren. Forgiveness is a powerful force. It's an act of generosity and love. It says a lot about Joseph that his betrayal became his blessing.

Perhaps the story of Judas is one of the most perplexing betrayals. Judas walked among the King of kings and the Lord of lords. Judas spent time with the One who did only good—healing people, resurrecting the dead, making miracles out of food, performing wonders, and loving those around Him. Yet, the most perfect One to ever live was betrayed by someone who knew Him well.

Isn't that the way it is? Those closest to us have the potential to hurt us the most. Those cuts hurt the worst. From our perspective, we can see that Jesus didn't cause the betrayal; instead, it was the selfish desires that were inside of Judas. When we are betrayed, we often search for what we did wrong. It rarely has much to do with us or who we are. It's really about who the betrayer is and what desires lie within them.

Those closest to us have the potential to hurt us the most.

....

In James 1:14 (ESV), we find these words: "But each person is tempted when he is lured and enticed by his own desire." In the case of Judas, it appears that his greed got the best of him. His desire for power and money is what drew him away. If he had only known that he had everything when he had a relationship with Jesus. Where were those initial thoughts and behaviors that could have been indicators that he was going to betray the Lord? We know from scripture that this betrayal had to take place; it fulfilled prophecy. But where were those red lights that someone most likely saw? Did Judas begin murmuring about his lack of resources, authority, or position? Did he try to get ahead in some other way? Was he talking with people he normally would have to go out of his way to engage? There was an origin of the thought and most likely some behavior—a sideways comment or deliberate action—that preceded ultimately selling Jesus out. We can always follow the trail backward to find evidence of the lie that entered into their heart.

As followers of Christ, we do not have to walk in shame, but we can learn from our past.

The list of biblical accounts of betrayal goes on and on, from Cain and Abel to Samson and Delilah all the way to Satan attempting to deceive all of mankind to this very day. When we read them and try to understand what was going on inside each of the people present—from the betrayer to the betrayed—we can see that what we think about ourselves and others is crucial to the success of our relationships. It is important whom we surround ourselves with and whom we turn to for advice. By relating the biblical experiences to our stories, we can discover behavior patterns that we may have overlooked and be more aware in the future so that we don't make the same mistakes. There is an old saying: "Fool me once, shame on you. Fool me twice, shame on me." As followers of Christ, we do not have to walk in shame, but we can learn from our past.

A worthless person, a wicked man, goes about with crooked speech, winks with his eyes, signals with his feet, points with his finger, with perverted heart devises evil, continually sowing discord; therefore calamity will come upon him suddenly; in a moment he will be broken beyond healing.
— Proverbs 6:12-15 (ESV)

Beloved, never avenge yourselves, but leave it to the wrath of God, for it is written, "Vengeance is mine, I will repay," says the Lord.
—Romans 12:19 (ESV)

Chapter 2

WHAT IS TRUST, AND WHY IS IT SO IMPORTANT?

To be trusted is a greater compliment than being loved.
— George MacDonald

Trust comes first. It even comes before a word is spoken in a relationship. Trust is hard to build and easy to break. It can be built over many years and lost in one instance. If someone in the relationship betrays or hurts the other, whether it is real or perceived betrayal, it brings into question all future actions. Many people say trust is even more important in a relationship than love. Trust is the foundation of a healthy, loving relationship, so you can't even have real love without trust.

Trust is defined as "the firm belief in the reliability, truth, ability, or strength of someone or something."[3] According to *Strong's Concordance,* in the Bible, it refers to being "bold, confident, sure, [or] secure" in someone or something.[4] It is something we all want from others, but it can be hard to give, build, and repair if it's broken. If trust is the foundation of every relationship, we should understand how we can take action to trust better. What we are going to learn is that trust isn't just built by one action or word; it's built by a million "little" things that add up to be incredibly significant. They either build tight bonds of trust or demolish them

King Solomon understood that little things can erode trust and become big things that steal our ability to build loving relationships.

---

3   "Trust: Meaning & Definition for UK English," *Lexico Dictionaries | English,* www.lexico.com/definition/trust.

4   *Strong's Hebrew:* 982, חָטַב (Batach)—"to Trust," biblehub.com/hebrew/982.htm.

He wrote to his bride, "Catch for us the foxes, the little foxes that ruin the vineyards, our vineyards that are in bloom" (Song of Solomon 2:15, NIV). In this picture, a beautiful vineyard isn't being destroyed by something big and obvious. It is by small foxes! In a vineyard, foxes don't just eat the fruit; they chew on the vines and dig holes around them which leaves their roots vulnerable to further damage.

Likewise, it isn't always the glaringly obvious relationship killers like cheating and lying that break trust. It can be a combination of many small behaviors like making excuses, not following through on commitments, overstepping boundaries, making negative judgments, revealing information that was meant to only be shared with certain people, being stingy with your words, possessions, or time, or just not living according to your values. Every interaction we have with people is either building or tearing at our trust levels. It is the foundation of every relationship we have.

Every interaction we have with people is either building or tearing at our trust levels.

. . . .

There are multiple types of relationships that require different amounts of trust. We don't have to trust every person with the same level of trust. Child-to-parent trust and parent-to-child trust require wholehearted investment. Romantic relationships and friendships require less. Trusting authority, government, coworkers and bosses, spiritual advisors, other drivers on the road, sales and business-people, and advertisers all require varying degrees of trust. We do not, nor should we, trust everyone at the same level.

If bonds of trust are foundational, we need to learn how to strengthen them because when they fail, the impact reverberates and touches us all. When they are cracked or broken, the relationship will eventually disintegrate. Think about the implications. Failing marriages affect everyone around them for generations to come. When relationships among government officials fail, thousands of people, families, and nations are impacted. It can result in war with all its ravaging effects. When businesses fail, it affects the local economy and all the families attached to that business directly and indirectly.

The negative effects on financial, emotional, physical, and relational well-being can be catastrophic. Even if a business is running, trust has a daily impact in the workplace. Paul Zak, in the *Harvard Business Review,* reports that when trust is high, positive results follow:

Compared with people at low-trust companies, people at high-trust companies report: 74% less stress, 106% more energy at work, 50% higher productivity, 13% fewer sick

*days, 76% more engagement, 29% more satisfaction with
their lives, 40% less burnout.[5]*

Trust affects every area of our lives and has complex implications.
The seven mountaintops of cultural influence are considered to
be family, religion, education, media, entertainment, business and
government.[6] If we can strengthen the foundations of trust in all
of those areas, can you imagine the kind of world we could live in?
If each person decided to become trustworthy and developed a
healthy relationship philosophy that they lived by, our foundations
would be impenetrable.

Pew Research Center has chronicled Americans' trust in their government since 1958. According to this research, in 1958, 73 percent
of Americans said that they trusted the government to do what's
right "most of the time."[7] Can you even imagine that? By the year
2019, that percentage had dropped fifty-six points to 17 percent. In
2014, Esteban Ortiz-Ospina and Max Roser looked at interpersonal
trust on a worldwide scale: 38 percent of Americans agreed that
"most people could be trusted." This was in direct contrast with
the percentage of people who agreed with that statement but
lived in other parts of the world like Romania (7 percent), Ghana

---

5   Paul Zak, "The Neuroscience of Trust." *Harvard Business Review*, 31 Aug. 2021, hbr.org/2017/01/the-neuroscience-of-trust.

6   "The Seven Mountains," *Generals International*, www.generals.org/the-seven-mountains.

7   "Public Trust in Government: 1958-2021," *Pew Research Center - U.S. Politics & Policy*, 28 May 2021, www.pewresearch.org/politics/2021/05/17/public-trust-in-government-1958-2021/.

(5 percent), Columbia (4 percent), and the Philippines (3 percent).[8] The study also showed that religion played a role in trust: Those who professed a religion were 2.6 percent more likely to trust others while people that attended religious services regularly and had a positive experience were an additional 20 percent more likely to trust.[9] Isn't it interesting that there is a significantly higher percentage of trust among people of faith?

Faith is defined in scripture as "the substance of things hoped for, the evidence of things not seen" (Hebrews 11:1, NKJV). It's a confidence that God will be true to His promises. Trust is a reliance on our faith. Trust is faith in motion. It could be that people who embrace the concept of a God who created all things, is omniscient, omnipresent, and can perform supernatural miracles and combine it with a personal commitment to love people and care for others in their community have a greater ability to trust. If you can trust in a big God, then trusting people isn't so hard because, even if they break you, you know He can heal you. When you know you are guided by God, then every experience you have—whether it is positive or negative—can be used by Him in your life to help you grow.

In her talk, "The Anatomy of Trust," researcher Brené Brown says that the ingredients of trust can be described by the acronym BRAVING:[10]

8   Esteban Ortiz-Ospina and Max Roser, "Trust," *Our World in Data*, 22 July 2016, ourworldindata.org/trust#:~:text=The%20World%20Value%20Survey%20allows,the%20bottom%20of%20the%20chart.

9   Ortiz-Ospina and Roser, "Trust."

10   Brené Brown, "SuperSoul Sessions: The Anatomy of Trust," *Brené Brown*, 25 Oct. 2021, brenebrown.com/videos/anatomy-trust-video/.

BOUNDARIES: *You respect boundaries, and when you are not clear about what is okay and not okay, you ask. You're willing to say no.*

RELIABILITY: *You do what you say you will do. This means you're aware of your limitations and don't over-promise. You are able to deliver on commitments and balance priorities.*

ACCOUNTABILITY: *You own your mistakes, apologize, and make amends.*

VAULT: *You don't share experiences that are not yours to share. You need to know that your confidences are kept, and, at the same time, you keep sensitive information about other people confidential.*

INTEGRITY: *You choose courage over comfort and what is right over what is fast, easy, or fun. You choose to practice your values rather than simply profess them.*

NONJUDGMENT: *You feel free to ask for what is needed and communicate those needs without judgment.*

GENEROSITY: *You extend the most generous interpretation possible to the intentions, words, and actions of others.*

In her extensive research, these are the "little" things she found that build trust ... the ingredients to building trust.

A *Harvard Business Review* article, "Re-Thinking Trust" by Roderick Kramer, says that several other factors are involved in trust. The chemicals in our body play a role. The level of oxytocin in our bodies directly correlates with the level of trust we have in someone. When people's levels of oxytocin were measured, they found more oxytocin was produced when the levels of trust were higher.[11] The more oxytocin we produce in a given situation or relationship the more we trust. We know that feelings are historically unreliable, so if we release oxytocin because of our feelings, it can cause us to trust poorly. Hugging, kissing, cuddling, and sexual intimacy can all trigger oxytocin production which can strengthen bonds. You can see how getting physical can blur the lines of trust, we can end up trusting people based on feelings alone, and our feelings can get us into trouble because they are not necessarily trustworthy.

The way we see others in terms of confirmation bias also plays a role. Confirmation bias is defined as "the tendency to interpret new evidence as confirmation of one's existing beliefs or theories."[12] In other words, we already believe something is true, and we find data that seemingly backs up our already existing belief. We all do this

---

11   Roderick M. Kramer, "Rethinking Trust" *Harvard Business Review*, 1 Aug. 2014, hbr.org/2009/06/ rethinking-trust.

12   "Confirmation Bias English Definition and Meaning," *Lexico Dictionaries | English*, www.lexico.com/ en/definition/confirmation_bias.

without exception. Belief systems are developed over time, and they are deeply rooted inside of us.

Belief systems are developed over time, and
they are deeply rooted inside of us.

....

I remember growing up believing that salesmen were all dishonest and were just trying to gouge people for money. Whenever my dad took me along to buy a car, I would feel uncomfortable thinking they were trying to take advantage of us. There were jokes made on television about car salesmen and even articles written about how people were ripped off which further deepened my bias. While it is true in some cases, not all car salesmen are dishonest. In fact, I know some pretty godly and upright ones—including my own cousin. We also have a friend who owns several car lots, and it seems as though everyone who buys the particular car make and model that he sells gets it from his dealership. They have built a reputation for fair prices and great customer service. They actually build long-term relationships with their customers through their service department.

There are honest and dishonest people in every arena because, well, people are there. To this day, I still feel edgy around salesmen and don't typically warm up to them when they try to make conversation and be personable. I am thinking, *You don't really care. You just want to sell this car. If I start talking to you, then, somehow, you are going to take advantage of me. You just want something from me.*

This was further driven home when we went to a "timeshare presentation update." We were up-front that we were not buying anything, but they insisted we just come listen to the "update" since we were already owners, and they needed us to know this new information. Just for listening to their presentation, they would give us a huge incentive like money or tickets to Disney. We thought, *Well, okay, free tickets sound great. After all, we have three kids!* Once we got to the sales table, we told the man we were not interested in buying but that his company had insisted we come anyway to hear about this update. He acted like he understood and began asking questions about each of us and what we did for a living. My husband began to talk to him about being in ministry, and the salesman said he was a Christian, too, and they shared some pleasant conversation about that. At the time, I was selling some skincare products, and I really enjoyed it, so I took the bait and opened up about my business. Big mistake.

After his big presentation, where he professed he would not be pushy, he did exactly the opposite. When we once again told him no to the new offers (the update was about new offers to buy more weeks), he became like Dr. Jekyll and Mr. Hyde. He transformed and began insulting me. He said, "Well, I guess your business isn't doing as good as you said it was." "You only came to get something for free, huh?" I was so in shock that he was being so nasty that I didn't know what to say. Of course, I had some ideas of what I should have said afterward, but it wouldn't have mattered at that point because the damage was done, and nothing I said would change that.

We left and gave him a negative review and guess what? We decided that we would never listen to another update—EVER—and we haven't in fifteen years. No sweet and honest salesperson will ever have a chance. We lost our trust. Maybe, like us, you have decided to never trust certain people, companies, organizations, or industries ever again. This is often substantiated by past evidence or experience but not always.

My childhood pastor used to tell the story of how his dad was friends with Sam Walton, the owner and founder of Walmart. Sam had asked his father to go in with him to start this company, and his dad declined. Can you imagine the regret he felt? Whatever his reason for declining, it all goes back to trust. When we hold onto stereotypes that are often false and act on them, it can be referred to as implicit bias. Implicit bias is when, instead of being neutral, we have an aversion to a certain group of people. Some stereotypes are often harmless but can become harmful when we act on them and make judgments and decisions based on them (explicit bias).

Research has shown that we tend to trust those who are most like us. There are a lot of people in the world that are not like us, so there is a good chance we are going to be more untrusting than trusting if we only trust those like us. According to Kendrick's "Re-Thinking Trust," we also hold to the illusion of invulnerability.[13] This means that we believe we have taken the appropriate steps and measures to not be vulnerable, and we've minimized risks, so we assume that we are safe. We believe we are right about our belief systems and whom we trust. Couple that with unrealistic optimism, and we have a recipe for pain. On top of all that, people can actually fake any indicator of trustworthiness, so how can we know for sure whom to trust?

We believe we have taken the appropriate steps
and measures to not be vulnerable, and we've
minimized risks, so we assume that we are safe.

We can start by trusting the One who is completely worthy of our trust. The One who designed and created us. Proverbs 3:5-6 (ESV) instructs, "Trust in the LORD with all your heart, and do not lean on your own understanding. In all your ways acknowledge him, and he will make straight your paths." When it comes to trusting others,

---

13   Roderick M. Kramer, "Rethinking Trust" *Harvard Business Review*, 1 Aug. 2014, hbr.org/2009/06/rethinking-trust.

we need to look both inward at ourselves and outward at others. This will help us spot and identify the traits of trustworthiness and untrustworthiness. Let's call them green lights and red lights. There are other times when we should proceed with caution. We'll call those yellow lights.

However, before we look at other people's traits, we need to look inside ourselves and examine the following areas:

» Our need for this particular relationship.
» Our track record in trust.
» Our expectations.
» Our values and our boundaries.

Once we have evaluated those, then we can look at trusting others. We must trust ourselves before we can trust others. The more confidence we have in our decision-making, the more we are able to place confidence in others. That confidence will come mostly from our relationship with God. He defines our value and worth, and when we know our true identity is from Him, we can walk in confidence.

WHEN EVALUATING OURSELVES, WE MIGHT ASK:

1) Do I have strong boundaries? Am I clear about my personal boundaries with others, and do I respect others' boundaries?

2) Am I reliable? Do I do what I say I am going to do? Do I over-promise and underdeliver? Or am I clear on my limitations and competencies?

3) Do I take responsibility for my actions, or do I blame others? When I make mistakes, do I apologize and make amends?

4) Do I share information that was meant only for me? Can others trust me to keep their confidential information?

5) Do I consistently choose to do what is right over what is fast, easy, or fun? Do I actually practice what I preach? Do my actions line up with what I say I value?

6) Am I honest with others about what I need, and can others be honest with me about what they need without worrying about judgment.

7) Do I believe the best about others' intentions, words, and actions?

8) Am I emotionally healthy?

9) Do I truly care about others, or am I more focused on my personal aspirations? Can I see the big picture?

Trust isn't just one thing; it has many ingredients.

When looking at both ourselves and others, we have to understand both the ingredients and the definition of trust. We have learned that trust isn't just one thing but that it has many ingredients. When trying to define trust, all the definitions have the same central meaning:

» It is how people feel when they know they won't be taken advantage of.

» Trust is feeling comfortable taking risks.

» Trust enables confidence and a willingness to take action on the basis of the behavior of another.

» Trust is the feeling that the goodwill of others who are making decisions is based on the good of all and not the gain of one.

» Trust is being comfortable depending on others, expecting them to do the right thing without monitoring or controlling them.

» The Oxford Dictionary definition is the "firm belief in the reliability, truth, ability, or strength of someone or something."14

» The Hebrew definition consists of faith, belief, confidence, fidelity, loyalty, trusteeship, allegiance, confidence, religion, and devotion.

» The Greek is translated similarly with the descriptors of confidence, trust, reliance, confidence, faith, credit, loyalty, belief, trust, conviction.

*Trust in the Lord with all your heart and lean not on
your own understanding; in all your ways submit*

---

14 "Trust: Meaning & Definition for UK English," *Lexico Dictionaries | English*, www.lexico.com/definition/trust.

to him, and he will make your paths straight.
—Proverbs 3:5-6 (NIV)

But blessed is the one who trusts in the Lord, whose
confidence is in him. They will be like a tree planted by the
water that sends out its roots by the stream. It does not fear
when heat comes; its leaves are always green. It has no
worries in a year of drought and never fails to bear fruit.
—Jeremiah 17:7-8 (NIV)

Chapter 3

WHOM SHOULD I TRUST? A TALE OF TWO VOICES: WHICH ONE DO I TRUST MOST?

Only after all the noise has spent itself do we begin to hear in the silence of our heart, the still, small, mighty voice of God.
—Aiden Wilson Tozer

Henry Wadsworth Longfellow is quoted as saying, "The human voice is the organ of the soul." Luke 6:45 (ESV) says that "The good person out of the good treasure of his heart produces good, and the evil person out of his evil treasure produces evil, for out of the abundance of the heart his mouth speaks." Our words indicate our beliefs. They are an open display of whose voice we have been listening to and whose voice we have become most familiar with. We become an echo of the voice we trust the most. We talk to ourselves throughout every day, and much of our inner dialogue has to do with how we were spoken to as children by those that were most significant in our lives.

Our words indicate our beliefs. They are an open display of whose voice we have been listening to and whose voice we have become most familiar with. We become an echo of the voice we trust the most.

Psychologists believe that by the age of seven, our belief systems are formed.[15] If our words indicate our beliefs, and our beliefs are

---

15 Carol Fox, "By the Age of 7 Most of Our Beliefs and Habits Are Formed," *LinkedIn*, 7 Mar. 2019, www. linkedin.com/pulse/age-7-most-our-beliefs-habits-formed-carol-fox#:~:text=Psychologists%20believe%20 that%20by%20the,of%20behaviour%20are%20being%20challenged.

formed by the words spoken to us at such an early age, then it is imperative that we make sure we evaluate our inner dialogue and are careful to choose what voices we continue to listen to, align with, and ultimately trust. Jesus would never speak to us the way some of us have been spoken to by others or even the way we speak to ourselves at times. What voice are we listening to?

John 10:4-6 (NIV) Jesus tells us something about the voice we should always trust. He says that He is the Good Shepherd:

> *"When he has brought out all his own, he goes ahead of them; and the sheep follow him because they know his voice. Buy they will never follow a stranger; in fact, they will run away from him, for they do not recognize the stranger's voice."*

Jesus told them this parable, but they did not understand what He was telling them. As I read this, I think to myself, *Doesn't it seem obvious what He is saying? Why didn't they understand? He is telling them that there are two voices calling out to the sheep. The Good Shepherd and the stranger. The Good Shepherd is the One who has been caring for, leading, guiding, protecting, and sacrificing for them. Of course, they should trust that voice. Why would they listen to a stranger telling them something different or causing them to question the Good Shepherd?* In this parable, Jesus is the Good Shepherd, and the enemy of our soul is the stranger. When either voice speaks to us, it sounds like our voice—our inner voice. The voice we resonate with the most is the one we have come to believe the most.

Just because we believe something doesn't mean that it is true. We must discern whose voice we are believing. One way we can discern which voice is speaking is to evaluate where their words will lead us since each voice is trying to lead us to a destination. We follow a voice. The question is, whose voice will we follow? God's voice is always leading us to fruitfulness and fulfillment that lasts. The enemy is leading us to destruction through the illusion of empty promises and quick satisfaction. Everything that our flesh desires is presented as an appealing image, but it delivers only temporary pleasure followed by a lifetime of pain.

We follow a voice. The question is, whose voice will we follow?

The enemy is referred to in the Bible as an angel of light. He makes everything look attractive, but it is a false image. It isn't an obviously false image. If he showed up with horns and pitchforks, we would immediately know to run the other direction. There is a reason he is called a deceiver. He deceives. You can only be deceived to the level you believe something to be true.

People who molest children don't usually show up and tell you what they are going to do. They don't walk around with kids on their t-shirts, their phone lock screens, and their social media, then hang out at the local playground leering at children. They are the family friend or family member that you didn't suspect. They were nice and kind or had some admirable traits or pretended to have them. The enemy comes in the form of a solution to a need we have. The light of what he has to offer (his deception) blinds us to the truth of his true motive. The deception is on the surface. If we can learn to wait a little longer, dig a little deeper, pray a little harder, discern a little more clearly, and follow the path of peace, we will not be so easily deceived.

The federal government in Canada trains its agents to spot counterfeit money by first studying the elements of genuine currency. Then, it is much easier to spot the counterfeit. In the same way, we will find that the more we know God's voice, His Word, and His principles, and are familiar with how well He cares for us, the more quickly we recognize an opposing voice. We can know God's voice through reading, meditating on, and obeying His Word, experiencing His presence in worship and prayer, and attentively listening to the teaching of His Word.

The voice of the enemy of our soul (the stranger) opposes God's will and appeals to our flesh. This is what trips us up. If there is a desire in us that we want instant gratification for or that we are desperate for, we tend to settle for the easy, quick, convenient, dazzling counterfeit. This is when we are most vulnerable to deception.

For example, think back to the beginning of a relationship that you have had that ended in betrayal. You probably wanted so desperately to believe in this person that you ignored every indication that they were untrustworthy even though the signs were right in front of you. When you looked back after the relationship you could name every warning sign, but you blew right past them when your desire for the relationship outweighed the pain of recognizing the truth about them. That is why they say hindsight is 20/20. We can see much more clearly when our emotions and desires aren't clouding our decisions. We have strong desires in our flesh. The only problem is that certain desires ultimately end in destruction.

The reason God hates sin is because it hurts and destroys His children. The enemy wants our destruction and pain, so he uses the desires of our flesh to lead us into destruction through temptation. What are these fleshly desires that we all have? They can be found in Galatians 5:17-21(ESV):

> For the desires of the flesh are against the Spirit, and the desires of the Spirit are against the flesh, for these are opposed to each other, to keep you from doing the things you want to do. But if you are led by the Spirit, you are not under the law. Now the works of the flesh are evident: sexual immorality, impurity, sensuality, idolatry, sorcery,

enmity, strife, jealousy, fits of anger, rivalries, dissen-
sions, divisions, envy, drunkenness, orgies, and things
like these. I warn you, as I warned you before, that those
who do such things will not inherit the kingdom of God.

The enemy wants us to settle for what SEEMS good. God wants
what IS good for us.

The enemy wants us to settle for what SEEMS
good. God wants what IS good for us.

If the enemy of our soul can appeal to our flesh, he can cause us to
put temporary trust in what he offers. Take sexual immorality, for
example. Arthur Zuckerman, based on a 2020-2021 general social
survey conducted in the United States, found the following:

» 20% of men engaged in an extramarital sexual affair and 15%
of women.
» 54% of the marriages immediately ended upon admission
of the affair.
» 30% more ended later and only 15.6% are still together.[16]

---

16 Arthur Zuckerman, "50 Cheating Statistics: 2020/2021 Demographics, Reasons & Who Cheats More,"
CompareCamp, 12 Feb. 2021, comparecamp.com/cheating-statistics/#:~:text=20%25%20of%20male%20
respondents%20reported,highest%20infidelity%20rate%20at%2031%25.

The cheating spouse never intended on destroying their family and going through the pain of divorce. That relentless voice just kept speaking over and over until the person was "led" into temptation.

The word "devil" is actually a compound of the words *dia* and *balos*. *Dia* is the root to diameter and means to pierce through. *Balos* means to throw an object like a ball or a rock. When *dia* and *balos* are together it means to repeatedly throw something until it penetrates its object. That's exactly what the enemy of our soul wants to do with his lies. Launch them at our minds like a ball over and over until the lies penetrate, and we believe them. A lie told often enough will eventually be believed as truth.

In His model prayer in Luke 11:4 (NIV), Jesus said to pray like this: "Lead us not into temptation." We cannot allow the enemy to lead us. He is a liar. In fact, he's the father of lies. He mixes a little truth with the lie in the hope that you will fall for his deception. He portrays an image of what will make you happy, but it is like a mirage; it lacks substance. At first, it does, but it's a temporary happiness at best. It rarely looks at long-term effects.

I remember talking with a young woman who wanted to end her marriage because she and her spouse had a highly emotional argument. I began to paint a picture of all the negatives she might face if she went down that road. "Are you going to be okay with your kids having a stepmom ... sharing holidays ... seeing your husband with another woman?" I asked. Eventually, she was able to see that her issue was solvable. In the end, giving in to temptation, could, ultimately, leave you broke, addicted, heartbroken, devastated, and disillusioned.

It's like the old billboards of the Marlboro Man. This handsome, rugged cowboy, who sat on top of a strong, magnificent horse, had a cigarette hanging out of his mouth. His subtle unspoken message was, *If you want to be like me, smoke this.* Never mind that he was only modeling and probably didn't even smoke. And, if he did, advertisers wouldn't show you the follow-up billboard a few years later when he was lying in a hospital bed, gasping for air, and dying of lung cancer. Everything the enemy traps you with makes you stay longer than you want to stay and pay more than you want to pay.

Everything the enemy traps you with makes you stay longer than you want to stay and pay more than you want to pay.

....

Take social media consumption into consideration. I have spoken to multiple teenagers who say TikTok and other apps became a full-on addiction consuming their lives. They started out casually using the apps, but soon the apps took over their lives. The statistics on cell phone and social media usage show a direct correlation with depression and anxiety. The constant comparison, the need to always be "on," the cyberbullying[17], the false information, teen tendonitis, sleep loss, stress, anxiety, risk of cancer, false prestige, obesity, and vision problems are major negative side effects of cell phone usage. Our flesh will always crave more of what we feed it. It is never satisfied.

Have you ever noticed almost everything we fall for is offered free at first? The first drink, drug, experience, or three-day trial on that app may be free at the beginning, but you will pay in the end. Sometimes, it can cost us everything—including our lives. We must evaluate the voice we choose to follow. God is faithful and trustworthy. He will never lead us to destroy our lives or the lives of others. That is why it is so important for us to focus on feeding our spirit over feeding our flesh.

> *"A stranger they will not follow, but they will flee from him, for they do not know the voice of strangers."*
> —John 10:5 (ESV)

The Stranger's Voice ...

Is Relentless

Is Accusatory

Questions motives

Gossips

Lies

Appeals to our selfish desires

---

17   Rachel Ehmke, "How Using Social Media Affects Teenagers," *Child Mind Institute*, 1 Mar. 2022, childmind.org/article/how-using-social-media-affects-teenagers/.

Starts small and free until we are in so deep it's hard to escape

Obsesses

Worries

Condemns

Discourages

Confuses

Pushes

Frightens

Rushes

This is in direct opposition to God's voice which we are to be led by as "followers" of Christ according to Romans 8:14 (NIV): "Those who are led by the spirit of God are the children of God." When we are familiar with God's voice, we can follow Him. His Word, according to Psalm 119:105 (KJV), is a "lamp unto [our] feet and a light unto [our] path" mapping the way forward for us to step not in darkness and confusion but on a path lit step by step. We have the inner voice of God's Holy Spirit guiding us.

In John 14:26-27 (author paraphrase), Jesus said:

> *"The Counselor, the Holy Spirit, whom the Father will send in My name, will teach you everything and remind you of all that I told you. Peace I leave with you. My peace I give to you. Not as the world gives do I give to you. Let not your heart be troubled, neither let it be afraid."*

When I am nervous or afraid, I feel physical pain in my gut. When I am happy, my gut feels lighter. Sometimes, we can't describe why we don't trust a person or a situation. We just have alarm bells going off in our gut. Some people say, "I've got this gut feeling," and interestingly, that is usually the place we "feel" God's voice guiding us. John 7:38 (BSB), Jesus said, "The one believing in Me, as the Scripture has said: 'Out of his belly will flow rivers of living water.'" Some theologians believe that is actually where the Holy Spirit resides. Regardless, His voice has certain characteristics, as listed below.

God's Voice …

Is loving

Calms

Convicts—Shows you where you've missed the mark but also shows you the way out. It is never condemning but always filled with hope.

Encourages

Enlightens

Leads

Reassures

Stills

Brings peace

Strengthens

Is Patient

Is Kind

Is Hope-filled

Lean in to the voice that loves you most. Know
that is the voice you can truly trust.

Lean in to the voice that loves you most. Know that is the voice you can truly trust. Imagine you are face-to-face with God, and He is speaking to you. His words would be filled with love and compassion for you. He has deposited His son Jesus inside of you, so He can only ever be pleased with what He sees when He looks at you. You carry His son. You reflect His nature. You are a new creation.

Chapter 4

THE SCENT OF TRUST

Trust thyself: every heart vibrates to that iron string.
—Ralph Waldo Emerson

H ave you ever heard someone say, "I can smell bull**** coming a mile away"? This means that they have a strong sense of when someone is lying. I'm not sure if you can smell dishonesty, but I am sure that you will always remember scents that are connected to particularly painful or joyful memories. Your brain may even seek connections with scents that have favorable memories for you.

There is a children's book by author Mem Fox called *Wilfrid Gordon McDonald Partridge*. Wilfrid lives next door to a retirement home and befriends ninety-six-year-old Miss Nancy. Everyone tells him she has lost her memory. Though he isn't even sure what memory is, he somehow helps her find it.

"What's a memory?" asked Wilfrid Gordon.

"It's something you remember," his father told him.

Dissatisfied, Wilfrid Gordon began to ask the old people in the home what a memory was.

"Something warm," said Mrs. Jordan.

"Something from long ago," said Mr. Hosking.

"Something that makes you cry," said Mr. Tippett.

"Something that makes you laugh," said Miss Mitchell.

"Something as precious as gold," said Mr. Drysdale.

Wilfrid Gordon went back home to look for memories. In a basket, he collected shells he had put in a shoebox, a puppet on strings, a medal his grandfather had given him, his football, and a nice warm egg, fresh from under the hen. Each item caused Miss Nancy to remember different stories in her life.

Memories are powerfully connected to trust, and scents are connected to memories. One of the signs of dementia is a loss of the sense of smell. Some of my relatives suffered from dementia, and I saw this first hand. I remember hearing a doctor say that if a person wanted to keep a check on their memory, they should go smell a lemon and make sure they can smell it. When we lose our ability to "smell" or sense dishonesty, we can get relational dementia— meaning we've forgotten how bad it hurt when we ignored the warning signs!

Memories are powerfully connected to trust,
and scents are connected to memories.

Millions of people got to experience what it was like to lose their sense of smell during the COVID-19 pandemic. People were very diligent to find ways to get it back again. I was one of them! It was very odd not to be able to smell for a few months. I wish I could gain my trust back as easily as I got my sense of smell back. You see, I am a little obsessed with beautiful scents and have been for as long as I can remember. In fact, I associate a lot of memories with scents, and I was inspired to write this poem titled "Scent of a Memory" when I was in college at the University of Georgia:

Scent of a Memory
The scent of a baby, fresh and new whispering softly, hear
her coo. The scent of a mother, tired and proud her nose
slightly powdered with a mashed potato cloud. The scent of
a puppy, happy at play rolling in the clovers and the fresh
stacked hay. The scent of evening, cool and dark crisp winds
are blowing in the nests of the lark. Countless memories
are brought back to the brim—when that scent so familiar
is pulled from within. Memories are tender, lovely and
sweet when that scent fills the air let your mind retreat.
—Charla Poole, 1993

I have always been fascinated with the connection between scent and memories. When I was a child, I loved the way Avon honeysuckle shampoo smelled in my hair as my sweet grandmother washed it in the sink of her white farmhouse-style home in Greenville, South Carolina. To me, it smelled like love, warmth, and summer vacation. If I get a whiff of anything like it today, it feels like a warm hug taking me back to my childhood. Love's Baby Soft and Musky Jasmine perfumes hold a special place in my heart, too, because my two closest friends and I doused ourselves in it day after day in high school. I have fond memories of my friends' 80s-styled bathrooms, loads of hairspray, and perfume clouds as we walked through the mist so it fell on us before heading off to school or on a night out of cruisin'.

There are plenty of other scents that have marked seasons of my life. Some feel like a punch in the gut because they take me to a place I would rather forget. Like the smell of a teen boy's cologne that takes me back to a night in high school when I was taken advantage of by a boy older and stronger than I was. He was stronger than my voice and stronger than my ability to break free. Why did I ever agree to go to his house? Sure, it was a double date, but we were the only two in his bedroom. I was humiliated and embarrassed, and I only told one friend. We both secretly hated him for it, but we never spoke of it again. He was an upperclassman and held a lot more clout in his social standing, and who would believe me? The decision to trust him because he was popular with other people would haunt me for years. Popular doesn't equal honest, kind, loving, or any other trait.

*Some scents feel like a punch in the gut because
they take me to a place I would rather forget.*

A lot of people can know someone on one level, but that doesn't mean they are trustworthy. If we just turn on the news, we can see multiple cases of "popular" people who end up being anything but the people we believed them to be. Just look at the "me too" movement. The traits of popularity, power, and wealth somehow caused people to be trusted more than they should have been. Thankfully, some brave women stood up and broke the illusion. They chose to stand up to power and popularity, and, now, those in power will, no doubt, be held to a higher level of accountability, and more women will be empowered to stand up for themselves.

The smell of chlorine reminds me of when I was twelve and home alone swimming with my older cousin. A knock at the door was followed by the entrance of an old family friend that I only saw from time to time. My cousin started acting completely out of character. She was bold and outspoken and smart usually. This day she was shaking, timid, and anxious. She jumped in the pool with her watch on, and this family "friend" offered to fix it. All I can remember is coming inside and sitting at our kitchen table with every piece of that watch lying on a towel. My cousin looked scared and horrified. I could tell she really wanted him to leave, but this watch project was keeping him there. The rest of the family finally returned home, and he left.

A lot of private conversations—that I was not a part of—happened that night. He returned the next day, and my dad met him outside. They were having a discussion in the garage, and I came out. For some reason, I jumped on the family friend's back. My dad was super mild-mannered, but he became enraged and told me to get down and go inside. I was so confused by his reaction. I later learned this guy had molested my cousin, and my dad was letting him know that he was never to return, and the authorities were being contacted. He later went to prison.

I thought about how oblivious I was to what was happening. I saw things that did not seem right or normal but did not know what to do with that information. Ignoring cues can get us in trouble with trust. I ignored the cues of my cousin's odd behavior, private conversations, my dad clearly not letting him in the garage, and becoming enraged when I jumped on his back. Now, I pay closer attention to body language, spoken words, settings of conversations, scents of important moments, and many other details. Just because a person is a friend, a friend of the family, is popular, or has a high rank does not mean you can trust them completely.

The metallic smell of a market in Moscow, Russia, and the hotel I stayed in on a mission trip there were enough to make you lose your appetite. The hotel was filled with Russian mafia and underground activity. The trip changed my life, but the smell turned my stomach and reminded me of the horror of Chernobyl and the hard lives of the precious Russian people I had the pleasure of meeting. I fell in love with the people but never that smell. I can only describe it like a handful of old pennies and nickels mixed with a musty attic, a burning wire, and radiation. It was not pleasant, but things that blow up other things should not get the privilege of a happy smell.

The orphanages we visited broke my heart. The director at the largest baby house in Russia told us that they do not teach the word "mother" to the children, but the children begin saying it anyway. Another orphanage that we visited was filled with very sad children. You could see it on their faces and in the way they carried themselves. They performed a few songs, and the smiles seemed forced at best. We brought treats, supplies, money, and games, shared the gospel, and left them with little salvation bracelets that consisted of different colored beads representing concepts like baptism, growing in their faith, love, and forgiveness. When we got ready to leave, we loaded the bus. A heaviness hung in the air. A little boy suddenly escaped the orphanage and ran onto the bus yelling, "Please take me with you! They beat us here!" We were all heartbroken.

The scent of that orphanage sticks with me. The feeling I experienced is still familiar. Sometimes you just sense that something is off. It's something you can't describe other than as a deep sadness and a heaviness. Despite the smiles and the songs they sang, the feeling lingered in the air. The appearance of happiness persisted, but it felt like a facade. We visited many orphanages; some of them did feel happy, the children seemed well taken care of, and we did not have that same feeling of uneasiness.

We are designed to trust as children. We are born little infants that are completely dependent on the adults who care for us (or don't care for us). The experiences we have early on can lead to specific perceptions of whom we can and cannot trust. Lack of care or abusive care can cause trauma and significant damage to our ability to trust. At the same time, when we are born into healthy, loving families, our ability to trust others is often higher.

The connection between scent and memory is a lot like the connection between trust and memory. Scents can provoke memories. Memories can provoke trust or distrust. The experiences we have with those we trust or trusted cause us to decide whom we will trust in the future. It's as though each human interaction shapes and molds our trust capacity. If a person named "Steve" hurts us, all Steves are now forbidden from being given our trust. A relative, a coworker, or a friend breaks our trust, and we suddenly find ourselves in fear of ever getting close to anyone who resembles the way Steve talked, looked, behaved, smelled, or spoke.

Trust is a tricky gift.

Trust is a tricky gift. If you give it to people of integrity, you get the satisfaction of a great relationship. If you give it to one who breaks it, you can be scarred for life, and, certainly, it affects every relationship in your future. What if I told you that there are keys I could give to you that unlock the secret doors that will help you find your way to more trusting relationships and warning signs that would keep you from trusting the wrong people. That would be worth a read for sure! Well, that is why you are here. Like me, you have trusted the right people and the wrong ones. My hope is that I can save you from making the same mistakes I have. I also hope you can take the hurts you have experienced and frame them in your mind in such a way that they no longer bring pain but wisdom, and you can one day see the betrayal you experienced as the gift that it is.

There is now hard evidence regarding the link between scent and trust. A study published in the journal *Frontiers* suggests that the calming scent of lavender is linked to interpersonal trust.[18] Aromas have been well-known to have an effect on our well-being; however, this is the first study that has found a direct link between a specific smell and trust.

There are more than two hundred references to scents in the Bible. God has given us some beautiful aromas to enjoy! He is very intentional with what he creates. When He gave us our five senses, it was intentional, and each has great importance. In the Bible,

---

18 Jasper H. B. de Groot and Monique A. M. Smeets, "The Subtle Signaling Strength of Smells: A Masked Odor Enhances Interpersonal Trust," *Frontiers*, 20 Aug. 2019, www.frontiersin.org/articles/10.3389/fpsyg.2019.01890/full.

scents are mentioned as perfume, ointment, incense, and balm. Their uses vary: medicinal, ceremonial, burial, and enjoyment are just a few. "Ointment and perfume delight the heart," according to Proverbs 27:9 (NKJV). Myrrh, frankincense, aloes, and cinnamon are mentioned in Song of Solomon 3:6 and Proverbs 7:17. Song of Solomon 4:11 (NASB) says, "Your lips drip honey, my bride; Honey and milk are under your tongue. The scent of your garments is like the fragrance of Lebanon."

Many times scents are associated with the memory of a person or an event. In Genesis 27:27 (author paraphrase), we see scent used for betrayal: "So Jacob drew closer to kiss his father, and Isaac smelled the scent of his son's clothes." Isaac was deceived by his senses. In this story, Jacob was wearing Esau's clothes which smelled like Esau, so their father would think he was Esau. Jacob's arms also felt like Esau's thanks to their mother, Rebekah, who was the author of this deception. I have to wonder if Jacob felt guilty every time he caught the scent of goat hair and the outdoors.

When it comes to our five senses—sight, taste, smell, touch, and hearing—we use all in communicating with others. We look at people's body language, physical appearance, how they smell, what words they say or don't say. All of these are important ways we collect information about another person as it relates to trust. We have often heard the adage, "Don't judge a book by its cover." I would agree. We need to dig deeper than the surface. Let's use all the senses afforded to us to discern, develop, and deepen our relationships. Let's practice using our "gut" by following the leading of the Holy Spirit as we explore our relationships.

Let's use all the senses afforded to us to discern, develop, and deepen our relationships. Let's practice using our "gut" by following the leading of the Holy Spirit.

Chapter 5

WHAT'S MY FILTER?

Naïve: showing a lack of experience, wisdom, or judgment.
—Lexico Dictionaries

There is a fine line between naivety and optimism; out of goodwill, some people tend to cross that line.
—Omar Sharif

I stumbled in the kitchen door, fell to my knees, and threw up all over the kitchen carpet. It was the summer of ninth grade, and I had just returned home from "summer school." That year, our county joined a neighboring county and held summer school at their location about thirty minutes away. My friend Tracey's dad had driven me, Tracey, and another friend home that day. He picked us up from school, but we had not actually attended school that day. At least not the kind that gave us an *academic* education. We had skipped school and gone to a party, or, more accurately, we had gone to someone's house to "party."

I had never partied like that. That was my first problem. The parties I grew up having were wholesome and clean. Good food, good friends, swimming, and games, and there was no alcohol ever. A guy we knew from school walked up as we got out of the car and invited us to a local party, and we drank beer. We went to a house and drank beer—some party! Why did we call that a party? Honestly, that's the only detail I remember. I don't remember having fun, food, games, or anything else. These little bottles called ponies were the drink of choice, and they were really gross, but I didn't want to miss out on what all these people said was fun. That was the first time I ever drank alcohol. On the way home, I felt like I was on a terribly evil carnival ride—the "Gravitron" to be exact. It moves around so fast that you are glued to the wall behind you while standing up.

I was dizzy and glued to the back seat with my two friends beside me while being chauffeured by Tracy's dad who kept glancing in the rearview mirror at me. I'm sure I was a sight to see. I could not wait to get home and get off this horrible "carnival" ride. Tracy's dad later told her, "That girl looked like she was drunk." He was right. I am sure he saw my eyes going 'round and 'round.

After I had fallen and left a mess on the floor, my mom walked in and said, "It smells like a brewery in here!" She didn't know how right she was. I told her I had eaten too many fruit roll-ups, and I was sick. What happened next I could not have anticipated. You see, the second problem is that we were scheduled to go to a family counselor that day for the first time, and I was going to be taking a series of tests. One was an IQ test and the other was the Rorschach Inkblot Test. My mom took an approach that she often did—"no excuses"—and we are going no matter what. She thought I was just nervous about the test, and that is why I was sick. But nothing was further from the truth.

We drove to the counselor's office in Atlanta, and I took the tests— drunk. I remember having to get up from the test and go to the bathroom to throw up. The results were analyzed, and we came back another day for the follow-up to get them. We walked into her office, and she began to go over the results. At one point, she said something that would frame my future:

"Charla, I am very concerned about you being taken advantage of. You are very naïve and trust people too easily. The way you interpreted the ink blots and the scenarios and conclusions you shared showed me that you only see the good in people and believe that their intentions toward you are good. This could put you in danger. In other words, the way you see life is not realistic."

As I look at Lexico's definition of naïve—"showing a lack of experience, wisdom, or judgment"—I believe all of this was true about me at that time. Since then, I have gained a lot more experience, wisdom, and sound judgment. Some may say the results of the tests were invalid because of the state I was in, but I think they were pretty accurate, and I have the life experience and track record to prove it. I have tried to analyze my past to see how I developed this way of looking at life.

Looking back, I can only be grateful for the way I was brought up. I was surrounded by a great family. I had a great church with so many positive encounters with people from authority figures to friends that I really deeply trusted people. From my perspective, most of the people really did want to help people and not hurt them. My world was a bit of a bubble: a squeaky-clean, fresh-smelling, light-and-airy, free-to-float, happy-song-singing bubble.

My world was a bit of a bubble: a squeaky-clean, fresh-smelling,
light-and-airy, free-to-float, happy-song-singing bubble.

I was aware that evil existed and that people could hurt others,
but I guess I was limited in knowing all the possibilities. My dad
worked at the United States Penitentiary—Atlanta, so I was aware
that people did bad things, and that is where they went if they did
them. He would tell story after story of the prisoners at dinner each
night. I guess I put a gaping separation between them and me; they
lived elsewhere, and no one I knew would ever do anything that
would land them in prison.

My dad was very protective of me, and I lived sheltered for many
years. He was always there watching and assessing the potential for
danger wherever we went. I didn't have to worry because he did
enough of that for us all. After all, he knew up close what humans
were capable of. I think he obsessed over all the possible dangerous scenarios daily. I once asked if we could get a convertible.
He said no, and I could never even ride in one because he saw a
news article describing how a couple had been decapitated when
they hit a bump and went flying in the air into electric lines. There
was no convincing him otherwise. For as long as I can remember,
he got up throughout the night—or at least once—to come into
my room with a flashlight and make sure I was still breathing. He

protected me. The adults in my life were supportive in every way. I was raised to trust.

The counselor's words were jolting and stuck with me, but what was I supposed to do? "Be careful" is not a real strategy. I needed tools—behaviors to look for—to help me know if I was vulnerable in certain situations, and I needed wisdom. Between ninth grade and now, I have made countless mistakes when it comes to trust. I still believe, at my very core, that people are mostly good. That belief has both served me and hurt me. My dad wasn't always around to protect me, and I had to learn what precautions to take.

I needed tools—behaviors to look for—to help me know if I was vulnerable in certain situations, and I needed wisdom.

That counselor was more right than she knew. I have been naïve and been taken advantage of more times than I care to admit, but I have also learned very much. I now have the pleasure of deep, fulfilling relationships, a great family, a tight circle of good friends, and, although I had some missteps along the way, I now know what to look for and how to avoid relationships that have the potential to break my heart with unnecessary suffering.

CHECK YOUR FILTERS

Belief System

Every person has a filter or a lens that they see life through. We refer to that lens as their belief system. Our belief systems are formed over time, mostly in our childhood, by our experiences, inferences, and deductions, or by accepting what others tell us to be true. According to "The Biochemistry of Belief," an article in the *Indian Journal of Psychiatry*:

> *Beliefs originate from what we hear - and keep on hearing from others, ever since we were children (and even before that!). The sources of beliefs include environment, events, knowledge, past experiences, visualization etc. One of the biggest misconceptions people often harbor is that our belief systems are an immovable, intellectual concept. Nothing could be farther from the truth! Beliefs are a choice. We have the power to choose our beliefs. Our beliefs [or filters] become our reality.[19]*

A person's belief system can then be described as a fixed mindset or a growth mindset. There has been a lot of research about having a fixed or a growth mindset. A fixed mindset says beliefs, intelligence, talents, skills, and other innate qualities are unchangeable. A growth mindset believes that those qualities can change and be developed. A fixed mindset will keep you limited by what challenges you.

---

19 TS Sathyanarayana Rao, et al., "The Biochemistry of Belief," *Indian Journal of Psychiatry*, vol. 51, no. 4, 2009., p. 239., doi:10.4103/0019-5545.58285.

When a growth mindset is embraced, challenges are enjoyable, and we strive to grow and learn. A growth mindset will empower your beliefs, so you can live a life that is limitless!

A fixed mindset will keep you limited by what challenges you. A growth mindset will empower your beliefs, so you can live a life that is limitless!

If you have a fixed mindset, you may believe, "I just pick all the wrong people in relationships!" What if you dug down to the root of that belief? What if you discovered you just didn't have the tools you needed to choose better relationships? Then, what if you discovered that those tools were available? Once you have the tools, you change your belief to "I am led by the Good Shepherd, and I choose the best relationships. In fact great relationships come to me." Your belief just went from limited to limitless. The good news is that as you become the best version of yourself, you actually *will* attract more great people into your life.

Wisdom and Knowledge
What knowledge do you trust? Where do you obtain it? A university? A set of authors? Those that claim to be experts in their field? Those

that theorize or those that have accomplished or built something? How you filter the wisdom and knowledge you embrace is critical.

This may be a little controversial. I hear people say they have a problem trusting the Bible or even certain versions of the Bible. People can have strong fixed beliefs about which version of the Bible is the only one you should read. There are those that have King James only beliefs. Others who will only vouch for the original Hebrew (Old Testament) or Greek (New Testament). I am sure people all have their reasons from accuracy to legalism. I tend to agree with my husband who says the best version is the one you will actually read!

When I am studying, I usually first look at the English Standard Version (ESV) which is a word-by-word translation. Next, I look at the Hebrew or Greek respectively. Finally, I look at The Passion Translation (TPT) which is poetic and The Message (MSG) which is more modern-day language. I get a deeper understanding from looking at several. I think I would miss out on the richness of Scripture and the context of the stories if I had a more rigid or fixed mindset. The whole point of Scripture is to help us to understand and engage the character, nature, and person of God. When I can see patterns, precepts, and principles, then I know I'm on the right path.

I understand when people say they don't trust the Bible or that it's filled with contradictions because I think, at some point, we all go through a crisis of faith. However, when we actually read the Bible and apply it to our lives, we can easily see the results, and they're always good! I remember going through such a crisis when I wasn't sure I could trust the Bible or church or even God. I began to study books like *Evidence That Demands a Verdict* and *More Than a Carpenter,* both by Josh McDowell, and *Experiencing God* by Henry Blackaby. Then, some events in my life led me to the undeniable truth that is stated so clearly in God's Word. Hebrews 11:6 (ESV) explains, "And without faith it is impossible to please him, for whoever would draw near to God must believe that he exists and that he rewards those who seek him." Oh, the rewards of knowing Him! Every person is on their own faith journey determining in whom and what they can really put their trust.

Oh, the rewards of knowing God! Every person is on their own faith journey determining in whom and what they can really put their trust.

Here are a few verses that display a glimpse into the importance the Bible places on our belief systems and how they are shaped:

» Romans 12:2 (ESV): Do not be conformed to this world, but be transformed by the renewal of your mind, that by testing you may discern what is the will of God, what is good and acceptable and perfect.

» Proverbs 30:5 (KJV): Every word of God is pure: he is a shield unto them that put their trust in him.

» Colossians 2:8 (ESV): See to it that no one takes you captive by philosophy and empty deceit, according to human tradition, according to the elemental spirits of the world, and not according to Christ.

» Romans 1:20-25 (ESV): For his invisible attributes, namely, his eternal power and divine nature, have been clearly perceived, ever since the creation of the world, in the things that have been made. So they are without excuse. For although they knew God, they did not honor him as God or give thanks to him, but they became futile in their thinking, and their foolish hearts were darkened. Claiming to be wise, they became fools, and exchanged the glory of the immortal God for images resembling mortal man and birds and animals and creeping things. Therefore God gave them up in the lusts of their hearts to impurity, to the dishonoring of their bodies among themselves....

» 1 Peter 1:14 (ESV): As obedient children, do not be conformed to the passions of your former ignorance.

According to the *Harvard Business Review* article "How Companies Can Profit from a Growth Mindset," a study was completed that cited research by Stanford psychology professor Carol Dweck relating to trust in business. In workplaces where a growth mindset was embraced, employees were:

- » 47% likelier to say that their colleagues are trustworthy,
- » 34% likelier to feel a strong sense of ownership and commitment to the company,
- » 65% likelier to say that the company supports risk-taking, and
- » 49% likelier to say that the company fosters innovation.[20]

Why would anyone want to keep a fixed mindset? If we are renewing our mind, that renewal will be a continuous process. We can even relate having a growth mindset to having faith. Just because we haven't seen something that we have hoped for come to pass in our lives doesn't mean it won't happen. If we can see it in our minds, then we can speak the promise. Eventually, we will see it come to pass if we are in agreement with God's will in faith. It only sounds like a dream or a fantasy until it actually comes true! Having a growth mindset demonstrates the beautiful relationship between faith, hope, and trust. Hope comes before faith. If we can have hope, then we can have faith, and our faith is connected to whom we trust to bring it to pass.

Hebrews 11 is filled with so much wisdom and even examples of great faith in action: "Now faith is the substance of things hoped

---

20 "How Companies Can Profit from a Growth Mindset," *Harvard Business Review*, Nov. 2014, https://hbr. org/2014/11/how-companies-can-profit-from-a-growth-mindset.

for, the evidence of things not seen" (Hebrews 11:1, KJV). And I love the poetic version of Scripture found in The Passion Translation:

Now faith brings our hopes into reality and becomes the foundation needed to acquire the things we long for. It is all the evidence required to prove what is still unseen. This testimony of faith is what previous generations were commended for. Faith empowers us to see that the universe was created and beautifully coordinated by the power of God's words! He spoke and the invisible realm gave birth to all that is seen.
—Hebrews 11:1-3

And without faith living within us it would be impossible to please God. For we come to God in faith knowing that he is real and that he rewards the faith of those who passionately seek him.
— Hebrews 11:6

But now God has invited us to live in something better than what they had—faith's fullness! This is so that they could be brought to finished perfection alongside of us.
—Hebrews 11:40

Actions

Our own trustworthiness also affects how we trust others. We tend to view others through the same filter we use to view ourselves. If we wouldn't, they shouldn't. If we would, they should. Counselors will tell you not to "should" people, and don't let people "should" you as you develop your boundaries. Decide what your core beliefs and values are, and structure your life around those. Place the boundaries around what you value. As you become true to yourself and your values, you become more trustworthy. The people in your life know what you stand for, and this is part of your integrity. The lens we see others through is made of immeasurable layers. As we discover how our relationships and beliefs have affected us and correct our lenses with truth, we can rightly see.

The lens we see others through is made of immeasurable layers. As we discover how our relationships and beliefs have affected us and correct our lenses with truth, we can rightly see.

Personality

Robert T. Sicora, a doctoral student at St. Thomas University, when conducting research for his doctoral dissertation, found some correlation between people with specific personality traits and their propensity to trust and be trusted.[21] He came to the following conclusions:

---

21 Robert T. Sicora, "Personality and Trust: A Qualitative Study on the Personality Styles/Traits of Leaders and Employees and the Impact on Culture of Trust within Organizations" (2015), *Education Doctoral Dissertations in Organization Development*. 43. https://ir.stthomas.edu/caps_ed_orgdev_docdiss/43

1) The more agreeable someone is the higher their propensity to trust.
2) The higher a person's emotional stability the higher their propensity to trust.
3) Introverted people are perceived as more trustworthy.
4) People who are cautious, precise, deliberate, detailed, objective, formal, caring, patient, relaxed, encouraging, non-confrontational are perceived as more trustworthy.
5) Social, demonstrative, enthusiastic, dynamic, friendly, spontaneous, strong willed, competitive, and determined people were seen as less trustworthy.

When you begin to look at any set of personality traits a person could have, you probably can see how specific types of personalities might be more prone to trust or distrust or be trusted or distrusted. As an extrovert, I read this and thought, *Yikes! I will just have to work harder on being a person of integrity. My actions will have to speak louder than my words.*

There are multiple personality tests or personal discovery tools out there that can be used to help us understand ourselves and others better: Myers Briggs, DISC, Life Languages, Enneagram, Strengths-Finder, and the list goes on and on. However, people also have varying degrees of trust when it comes to personality tests.

It all goes back to our belief systems. Some people don't trust these tests' validity or accuracy. You could get out of balance if you misused them, but if you are able to "eat the meat and spit out the bones"—take what you need and discard what you don't—a lot can be gained. One of the personality tools that has helped me so much in relationships stirred up a heap of controversy from (I choose to believe) well-meaning people. I was attacked online when I mentioned it and even had people make snarky comments like "Do your research," or "It's just like a horoscope. What's wrong with you? You are a pastor's wife!" They never stopped to think that maybe I *did* do the research and came to a different conclusion than they did. We just have different viewpoints. The comments were judgmental at best and rude and disrespectful at worst.

It is interesting how we can become so sure of our beliefs that we become self-righteous. We trust our beliefs so much that we believe being right is more important than loving people well. People tend to judge others when self-righteousness sets in. However, when we realize that none of us deserves the grace we have been given, we can be anything but self-righteous. Jesus paid it all, and we did absolutely nothing to earn it. We are all in desperate need of His mercy and grace. If we can't express ourselves in any given area with love, it's more than likely a reflection of our inability to receive God's love in that area.

At the end of my life, I hope above everything that people say about me that I loved well. It's the most wonderful attribute of God and something that is His very nature. I want to fully embrace His love, so I can have a deeper relationship with God. Then I can pour it out on others. Regardless of whether others believe the same thing we do or not, the chief identifying mark of a believer is that they love others. No matter what trust you have in your beliefs about life and relationships, I encourage you to remain humble and open to learning.

At the end of my life, I hope above everything
that people say about me that I loved well.

....

Can you identify your belief systems? You can find tools that ask specific questions to help you online. A good counselor (which I highly recommend for *everyone*) can also help you to identify them as well. You may even have a good friend that can help you discuss and challenge them.

Many times when you have a strong opinion or make a strong statement, you can ask yourself: *Who said that? Why do I believe that? Is it true? Is it helping me move my life forward? Is it benefitting my relationships?* We all have common core beliefs. When we can identify them and get to the root, we grow, feel better about ourselves, and have better relationships. We often need help to identify them because we don't even realize some of them are guiding our decisions. As one of my mentors Pastor Keith Craft says to me: "You have to think about what you think about! If you can elevate your thinking you can elevate your life!"

LIMITING OR FIXED CORE BELIEFS

I need to earn happiness.

I need to control my environment to manage my feelings.

The world is a dangerous place.

Even my best efforts are not good enough.

If someone gets to know me, they won't like me.

I can never count on anyone but myself.

Men cannot be trusted.

Friendships with women are too hard.

You shouldn't have more than one close friend.

GROWTH MINDSET CORE BELIEFS

I can be happy without having to earn it.

I am able to manage my emotions because I have the Spirit of God inside of me.

The world may be dangerous, but I am strong enough to face any adversity.

I give my best and forget the rest! I am on a continual journey of improvement.

Everyone may not like me, but those meant for my life will love me!

I am trustworthy, and I choose to surround myself with trust-worthy people.

I will give everyone a fair chance to be trusted.

Female friendships are rich and supportive, and I am adding to my tribe more and more.

I can have as many close friends as I choose to.

Our filter consists of our belief systems. Check, evaluate, and adjust your systems to make sure you are believing the truth. Then, your life and your relationships can thrive. What is your filter?

> *Do not be conformed to this world, but be transformed by the renewal of your mind, that by testing you may discern what is the will of God, what is good and acceptable and perfect.*
> — Romans 12:2 (ESV)

Chapter 6

WHEN TO STOP, YIELD, OR PROCEED (RED, YELLOW, GREEN LIGHTS)

When someone shows you who they are,
believe them the first time.

—Maya Angelou

THE HEDGEHOG PRINCIPLE

One cold winter's day, a number of porcupines huddled together quite closely in order, through their mutual warmth, to prevent themselves from being frozen. But they soon felt the effect of their quills on one another, which made them again move apart. Now when the need for warmth once more brought them together, the drawback of the quills was repeated so that they were tossed between two evils, until they had discovered the proper distance from which they could best tolerate one another. This demonstrates the need for society that springs from the emptiness and monotony of life alone. It causes them to be driven together but their many unpleasant and repulsive qualities and insufferable drawbacks once more drive them apart. The mean distance which they finally discover, and which enables them to endure being together, is politeness and good manners. Whoever does not keep to this, is told in England to 'keep his distance.' By virtue thereof, it is true that the need for mutual warmth will be only imperfectly satisfied, but on the other hand, the prick of the quills will not be felt. Yet whoever has a great deal of internal warmth of his own will prefer to keep away from society in order to avoid giving or receiving trouble or annoyance.[22]

---

22 Arthur Schopenhauer, "Chapter XXXI, Section 396:[1]." *Parerga and Paralipomena*, vol. 2 (London: Clarendon Press, 2000).

There has been psychological research done around this principle and even a short film produced in 2015 where a hedgehog who loves to hug continues to hurt others until he eventually befriends a turtle who, due to his impenetrable shell, cannot be hurt by the hedgehog's quills. It's a film that is both cute and meaningful. If we compare our lives to the film, we are all a little bit like hedgehogs. We have unhealed areas of our lives and weaknesses that poke and hurt others and vice versa. We are fortunate when we find those in our lives that are tough enough to withstand our weaknesses (quills). In every relationship, we run into each other's quills from time to time resulting in pain. When we are hurt, we have a choice in how we will respond. Hopefully, we don't remain like hedgehogs that continue to injure each other over and over every time we get close.

We are fortunate when we find those in our lives that are tough enough to withstand our weaknesses (quills).

....

Everyone has experienced hurt, and unless that is healed, it can cause us to act in less than wonderful ways toward others. The goal is healing, and the more healed we are, the more likely we are to stop the cycle of pain. Healing comes when we can acknowledge our pain, allow God into that space, allow another healthy person that has our best interests into that space, and we listen. We listen to God's Word, His Spirit, to that trusted healthy person, and we listen to ourselves. Then we find new and better ways to communicate our desires, hurts, frustrations, and boundaries. We learn things about us that will help us grow into the best versions of ourselves when we take the time to listen.

We each have different personality traits that some find endearing and others find repelling. We have behaviors that are either driving our relationships closer, or they are tearing them apart. In a healthy, trusting relationship, each person does more of what drives their connection to be deeper, and they avoid behaviors that drive it further apart.

The repellant behaviors that tear and drive relationships apart are what I call "red lights." I am not saying that the presence of negative behaviors means relationships should immediately end—with the exception of any type of physical violence or other form of abuse. If that is ever present, then that relationship should either end immediately or you should separate from it until the person that is abusive gets help and is healed. God loves His children, and He never condones abuse. There is no excuse for abuse. What we are looking for with the red lights is a consistent pattern of behavior.

When we look at this list of toxic behaviors, we may recognize some of them in ourselves or others. Self-awareness is a key to changing these in ourselves. We can never change another person, but we can change ourselves and protect ourselves from hurtful people. There is a Bible reference that talks about writing the vision and making it plain. What I have experienced when talking to others is that many people have never had a true model of a healthy relationship, so it's most difficult for them to have a vision for what it is supposed to look like. They are either too perfectionistic with others, or they accept terrible treatment thinking that it is "normal," and they have what they deserve. We are all worthy of loving and trusting relationships. So let's look at these behaviors as major warnings that trouble is ahead if we continue in a relationship where these behaviors are present.

I have heard the before marriage advice that if you get to know someone through seasons you will see better how they respond to pressure. Many of our quills pop out under pressure. That is why it's good to take your time before committing to a lifelong relationship. Get to know the person you want to spend forever with in different environments and through a few seasons.

THE ROOT REVEALS THE FRUIT

If these behaviors are present in someone, there is probably unaddressed pain or trauma in their life. These behaviors are some of the fruit of their lives. If you don't like the fruit you are seeing now, it will only get worse unless the person takes responsibility for their actions. The root of the red light behaviors is most likely pain. It is neither your responsibility to change the fruit nor can you. It is also not your responsibility to heal the root. God may use you to help heal, but that is up to Him. He is the ultimate healer. You can recognize it, be aware of it, pray for them, give them godly counsel, and ask them to get the help they need, but you may want to discontinue forming a close relationship with a person who demonstrates any of these behaviors consistently.

God may use you to help heal, but that is up to Him. He is the ultimate healer.

....

RED LIGHTS

What do you do when you see a red light? Well, hopefully you stop. This list of characteristics is meant to help you recognize specific behaviors in both yourself and others that, if not healed can cause immense and unnecessary pain.

Is secretive

Projects behaviors onto you that they themselves demonstrate

Is easily angered

Becomes uncontrollably angry (may be frequent or infrequent but is a pattern)

Allows anger to seethe then blows up

Is unable to control emotions

Is inconsistent in multiple areas of their life (job, finances, hygiene, fitness, education, responsibilities, relationships, words, etc.)

Speaks negatively about others

Is in a constant state of strife and can't be at peace

Argues

Insists on the last word and has to be right

Is unable to listen to opposing viewpoints and has a fixed mindset

Does not respect boundaries (oversteps them, blows up when you try to set them)

Is unreliable

Shares private information about you or themselves with others without your permission & knowledge

Is judgmental of others

Is extremely opinionated

Gets vocal about their opinions but is unwilling to listen to other viewpoints

Is unaware of how their actions impact others

Doesn't take responsibility for their own actions and blames others instead

Withholds their belongings and/or feelings

Knows a great deal about others but isn't as open about themselves (nosey)

Constantly changes friends and groups and has very few or no long-term friends

Gaslights others (makes them question their own sanity, perception, reality)

Doesn't trust others and is often suspicious

Puts on a facade that everything is ideal in their life

Lacks real empathy (They say they care, but their sincerity is lacking.)

Is consistently hurtful and negative

Controls

Manipulates

Few others speak well of them (reputation)

Is deceitful and lies (Everyone tells untruths at times, but this is a consistent pattern and how they deal with their problems.)

Turns the tables in conflict and makes issues about you

Makes you feel incapable or weak

Causes you to feel dependent on them and their approval

There is a disconnect between who they think they are and reality

Resorts to insults and name-calling when they do not get their way

Blames you for their negative behaviors

Tries to hide their weaknesses by focusing on your weaknesses instead

Is defensive

Becomes upset or angry, unable to hear your concerns and unwilling to take responsibility for their actions

Acts self-righteous

Projects insecurities and flaws onto others

Elevates themselves above everyone else

Refuse to see their own negative qualities

Apologizes without changing their behavior

Expresses regret in various ways but nothing changes

Avoids their issues

Blames others for their issues instead of admitting they have a problem or taking steps to help their issue

Finds fault in others

Fails to forgive others for their mistakes

Flatters you instead of talking to you about concerns they may have with you

Demands trust instead of earning it

Shows inconsistent care for you (One day they care; the next day they don't.)

Takes offense when you don't trust them immediately

Refuses to grow and improve

Draws you away from God

Isolates you from friends and family

Expects perfection

Shows an inability to connect

Domineers others

Is constantly defensive

Is in denial

Steals

Cheats in the small things

Is abusive, addictive, greedy, spiteful, vengeful, lazy, lustful, egotistical, rebellious

Makes you constantly uncomfortable by doing things incongruent with your values

Any of these characteristics is a red flag, whether it appears in a romantic relationship or with a friend, family member, or coworker.

No one is perfect, and change takes time. But if you notice that someone is resistant to hearing your concerns, becomes angry or defensive, blames you for their behavior, and does not show signs of wanting to change, you have to either proceed with caution or end that relationship knowing that there are others out there who will treat you with respect.

One red light that I want to bring particular attention to is out of control emotions, especially anger. I have seen too many women hurt and even killed at the hands of someone they loved but who never learned to get their anger under control.

> *Make no friendship with a man given to anger,*
> *nor go with a wrathful man, lest you learn his*
> *ways and entangle yourself in a snare.*
> —Proverbs 22:24-25 (ESV)

I was in third grade at a new school that I loved! Every day we walked in and got a carton of milk. You could even have chocolate if you wanted it. One particular day, I was so excited to chug that milk, and, wouldn't you know, that was the day the milk came out in chunks! Gross! It stunk, it made me gag, and it turned my stomach. It's almost the same reaction I have to people who cannot control their anger. Their voice starts to change. Their face begins to contort. The aggression begins, and I have a few reactions: shrink back, run away, cry, or fight back. None of these changes the outcome for the person who is out of control. Some people learn to use their anger as a tool to get what they want. They manipulate others into submission using anger as their weapon.

Make no mistake; anger is a powerful emotion. It can cause people to do things they never thought themselves capable of. Angry people are fearful people. It sounds contradictory, doesn't it? Fear makes us feel out of control so we use anger to get control and feel powerful, but it is an illusion of control. When we experience trauma in our lives, it's usually an area we have felt like we had no control over. Something was either done to us or not done for us. It creates fear. That fear unchecked can result in anger, and that anger can be channeled into a form of control. If someone can control you, they seemingly get what they want although it's usually temporary. If they yell, scream, give you the silent treatment, or call you disparaging names, they are out of control and using these tools to try and control you. It's abusive, wrong, and unhealthy for both them and you.

I have seen big, muscular, take-charge people who would fight anyone be completely and utterly at the mercy of fear. That fear is channeled into anger. It's a form of control. It's the only thing that gets them what they think they want. As crazy as it sounds, I once was hanging out with a group of high school friends, and there was this one guy that always scared me in the group. He was muscular and big and loud. He was also very sweet to me and all the girls in the group. Like really sweet, but he was always fighting with guys, and I don't just mean with his words. It was like he carried a boxing ring in his back pocket. One night we were cruising down the strip in Panama City, Florida, and this guy, driven by his inner rage, jumped out of the car, poured a bucket of urine on and beat up some poor guy who was just innocently walking down the road. We were yelling, asking him to stop, but he was on autopilot. I cried, and we all just sat there in disbelief. Needless to say, I never intentionally chose to be around him ever again.

Another time, this guy banged his head into a Volkswagen windshield until he was covered in blood and flipped the car over. He had no idea whose car it was. He was just upset, and that was the target. Clearly, this is an extreme example but unfortunately not as rare as we might think. Some of this particular guy's issues revolved around his use of steroids, but most of it came from a home life where abuse was prevalent but hidden. I did not learn about his home life abuse until much later.

Many times, we have no idea what is happening in the private lives of others; however, when we see extreme behaviors, they are an indicator there is some underlying pain that has not been healed. When I look back, he was waving a huge red flag saying, "Somebody, please help me!" but we neither had the maturity nor the tools to help him. I was able to see him later in life, and he seemed to be doing much better, but, sadly, he died a few years back—too young. He was in some type of altercation that led to his untimely death. I watched girl after girl pursue a relationship with him, and inevitably they did not work out. Why? It may have been that the scars were deep, and the pain was never healed.

Many times, we have no idea what is happening in the private lives of others; however, when we see extreme behaviors, they are an indicator there is some underlying pain that has not been healed.

....

They say when you really want to see a person's character put them in a pressure situation over the course of time, and see how they respond. That doesn't mean they have to be perfect. Let's be real here; we all lose control of our emotions on occasion, but is it our pattern? Is it their pattern? If so, it's a red flag waving in our face. It will not get better unless they, themselves, decide to go for help. We can't force it or make it happen. We certainly do not need to share intimacy in any form with a person who cannot consistently control their emotions. Anger can be constructive or destructive. If you have trusted your emotions to an angry person, I pray you learned valuable lessons from the relationship, and you have found healing. Most importantly, I pray you discover why you chose to trust them and what it was in you that was drawn to them.

I look back in my life at one particular relationship where anger and control were prevalent, and for me, I think it was just wanting—in my own life—the strength they had. I felt weak, I perceived them as strong, and somehow I got twisted in my mind that the reason he wanted to control me was that he loved me. He did love me in the best way he knew how, but it was unhealthy, and I often found myself crying and in emotional turmoil.

This principle is not limited to romantic relationships. It applies to friendships, work relationships, parental relationships, and any relationship. Out of control anger is abuse, and there is never an excuse for abuse. We can understand and be empathetic but never have real relationships with those who cannot control their anger. When we look at the Bible, we can see anger displayed in King Saul, Cain, Moses, Balaam, King Ahab, Haman, Esau, Absalom, and Jezebel. Only one of them that we know of repented and had healthy relationships afterwards. People who are *truly* powerful do have control over their own emotions, and they do not blame their angry outbursts on the behavior of others. True strength is found in patience and kindness. Maybe you are trusting someone now with out-of-control anger. I urge you to consider the following scriptures:

» James 1:19-20 (NIV): My dear brothers and sisters, take note of this: Everyone should be quick to listen, slow to speak and slow to become angry.
» Proverbs 29:11 (NIV): Fools give full vent to their rage, but the wise bring calm in the end.

» James 1:20 (NIV): Human anger does not produce the righteousness that God desires.

» Ecclesiastes 7:9 (NIV): Do not be quickly provoked in your spirit, for anger resides in the lap of fools.

» Colossians 3:8 (NIV): But now you must also rid yourselves of all such things as these: anger, rage, malice, slander, and filthy language from your lips.

» James 4:1-2 (NIV): What causes fights and quarrels among you? Don't they come from your desires that battle within you? 2 You desire but do not have, so you kill. You covet but you cannot get what you want, so you quarrel and fight. You do not have because you do not ask God.

» Proverbs 22:24 (NIV): Do not make friends with a hot-tempered person, do not associate with one easily angered.

» Proverbs 14:29 (NIV): Whoever is patient has great understanding, but one who is quick-tempered displays folly.

» Proverbs 16:32 (ESV): Whoever is slow to anger is better than the mighty, and he who rules his spirit than he who takes a city. (The stronger you are the better you control your emotions—author interpretation)

» Proverbs 22:24-25 (NASB): Don't befriend angry people or associate with hot-tempered people, or you will learn to be like them and endanger your soul.

Many young women in a relationship with someone out of control of their emotions have told me, "But he has this other side that is so kind." While this may be true, it does not negate the abuse. If someone really loves you, they will take responsibility for their own actions and get help. This is not dependent on you. It is not your fault that they lose their cool. Every person is responsible for their own behavior. No one else needs to take the blame for them.

We all deal with anger. It's how we respond when we are angry that makes all the difference.

....

We all deal with anger. It's how we respond when we are angry that makes all the difference in whether we hurt others or ourselves or if we are recognizing that it's an indicator, and it is showing us something deeper. This may require us to take action, but, sometimes, it requires us to take *no* action. In my own life, I have found that anger is sometimes a secondary reaction to something else like rejection or not being taken seriously. Other times, it's the primary emotion. Either way, if I can relax, take some deep breaths, evaluate my anger and find out what that is telling me, let time pass, or just go limp, I will handle my anger better. I always regret when I am quick to react instead of pausing to respond.

I used to read a book of proverbs to my children that contained the verse below. An illustration in the book was of an angry person that had smoke coming out their ears. Their mouth was wide open like they were yelling. Their fists were clenched as they were stomping their feet!

Do not make friends with a hot-tempered person, do
not associate with one easily angered, or you may
learn their ways and not be able to change.
—Proverbs 22:24-25 (NIV)

YELLOW LIGHTS: PROCEED WITH CAUTION

A yellow light would be anything in the red light list that is infrequent (with the exception of abuse) but is a cause for you to be concerned. It causes a gut feeling that you cannot shake and/or if you are head over heels for this person. When your need for the relationship is high, you may overlook red flags, so proceed with caution. Be aware, and give it time.

God wants you to be able to recognize character problems (red lights) for two reasons. One is to be able to confront each other with the truth so that we can see our faults and overcome them (Galatians 6:1 and Matthew 18:15-18.) We are to be redemptive agents in each other's lives. The second reason is for our own protection and growth. If someone is unwilling to change or grow, and we are committed to changing and growing, it may be time to reconsider the relationship. Invite someone you respect that has good relationships in their life to help you evaluate the relationship dynamics.

If you are unsure, invite a trusted friend into the conversation. Pray for God to show you whether you should proceed or end the relationship. Then, follow the path of peace. You can avoid much unnecessary pain if you will use these tools to help you. Be intentional about your relationships. There is nothing worse than staying in a toxic relationship and nothing better than having healthy relationships!

GREEN LIGHTS: GO FOR IT!

These green light attributes are wonderful and special! When you find these qualities in people, you have struck gold and found true treasure.

> *As iron sharpens iron, so a friend sharpens a friend.*
> —Proverbs 27:17 (NLT)

Helps you be your best
Encourages you
Helps you develop other healthy relationships
Encourages you to be all God designed you to be
Is open and vulnerable
Welcomes feedback, expressions of concern, and even criticism, especially by people who love them
Is humble
Apologizes when wrong and follows that with behavior change. Changes not because they feel they have to, but because they truly want to get better, and they want the best for the other person
Expresses concerns about you because they care about you
Is kind, patient, emotionally intelligent, steady and consistent

Communicates thoughts and emotions

Is reciprocal

Invests in the relationship

Is committed to getting better

Is industrious

Keeps commitments

Speaks well of others

Speaks words of life and positivity

Respects your boundaries and feelings

Is reliable, generous, confident, and sure

Has a growth mindset

Displays care and empathy

Maintains healthy relationships

Has long term friendships

Takes responsibility for their own actions (owns their mistakes)

Forgives easily

Knows their worth and value come from God

Committed to growing and being their best

Is not threatened by your success

Gives others the benefit of the doubt

Is positive, peaceable, grateful,

Does not anger easily

Controls emotions

Speaks positively about others

Respects boundaries

Keeps your secrets

Is open to others' thoughts and ideas

Cheers for others

Has long term friendships and healthy relationships

Shares their struggles

Fights fair

Has a servant's heart (nothing is beneath them)

Loves well

Kindly confronts and challenges you to be better

Were you able to identify some of these traits in yourself? I hope so. If you have some that you want to improve, choose one, and work on that area of growth.

Recognizing which lights are telling us to stop, pause, or go will help us end potentially harmful relationships before they start. This minimizes unnecessary pain and will help us move freely toward those that will provide deep, meaningful connections.

Chapter 7

TRUST PRINCIPLES

*Better to trust a man who is frequently in error
than the one who is never in doubt.*
—Eric Severeid

NOT ALL-ENCOMPASSING

Trusting someone in one area doesn't mean you can trust them in all areas. You wouldn't ask your banker to do what only a surgeon could do. You wouldn't ask your lawyer to bake your wedding cake. You wouldn't ask your florist to preach your funeral. Everyone is a ten at something and maybe even a few things. We all have our areas of expertise. Similarly, just because someone can be a trusted friend doesn't mean they will be a trustworthy business partner. In relationships, you grow to learn what level of trust you can place in a person in different areas.

I used to love going to the county fair! The smell of popcorn, funnel cakes, bubble gum, and candy apples would amp me up! I loved the games . . . and the rides . . . all of it! When I was in college, there was a local fair, my boyfriend invited me to go, and I was out the door, ready for a fun night. We were enjoying all the festivities when we saw this billboard that said, "World's Tiniest Woman." I looked at him with my eyes wide and said we had to go see her! Visions of a childhood book *Thumbelina* popped into my head. My dreams as a child consisted partly of having my own Thumbelina or a little fairy that would be my own little friend. As an only child, she would take the place of my sister. So . . . of course, I wanted to see her.

He looked at me, and even though he didn't know about my child-hood dreams, he somehow discerned enough to say, "I don't think it's going to be what you are thinking, and I don't think you are going to like it." I could think of no possible scenario that would cause me to be unhappy with this choice. What in the world was he even saying? Oh, how I wish I had listened! We stepped up into this small, musty metal trailer, and there she sat behind a half-circle of railing that was like a small barrier between her and us. She was far from my Thumbelina dreams. She wasn't the smiling, happy, ready-to-be-my-friend kind of tiny woman. Instead, we, along with about ten other people who gawked at her and just moved along, were trapped in a scenario I'm sure none of us were ready for. I'm sure we all got the sinking feeling that this was so very wrong.

What we saw was a woman, literally, about 1-1/2 feet tall. She may have come up to my knee cap, and I'm only 5'5". I promise I am not exaggerating. She was very old and had a tiny chair, a spittoon (to spit her tobacco chew in), and a can with dollars in it. She had a scowl on her face as if to say, "Yeah, look at me. I know you think I'm a freak!" She hit that can with her little cane and never even looked up at us. She seemed so miserable. I was a wreck. We walked out, and I just cried: "Why is this here? Why is this allowed? It's so sad and horrible, and we just participated in exploiting this person." I cried, and he looked at me and said, you guessed it, "I told you so!" I looked right back at him and thought, *I sure wish you had provided some details and context!* although I'm not sure I would have listened. I should have trusted him in that instance. His advice was right on.

When it comes to trusting someone's advice, one question we should ask ourselves is this: Who does this stand to benefit most?

When it comes to trusting someone's advice, one question we should ask ourselves is this: *Who does this stand to benefit most?* While we cannot presume to determine the motives of another person, we can ask ourselves, *Does this benefit them most or me?* Sometimes it's a win-win situation, and we both benefit. Sometimes, only they benefit, or they benefit *most*. Other times, they are simply looking for you to benefit even to their own loss. In this case, he was trying to protect me. He had nothing to gain or lose, but he knew my heart would break. There were other instances I shouldn't have trusted him, and that makes trusting others cloudy and confusing. Certain things they say or do can be trusted but others not so much.

So how do you know if you should enter or stay in a relationship with someone whose trust rating is questionable, erratic, or just spotty? I have heard the statement that "the way you do anything is the way you do everything." While I believe that statement to be mostly true, I disagree that it is an absolute truth. I know people who are meticulous at numbers and finances and their desks are neat as a pin, but their closets and car are a wreck. We need to look at the *overall* patterns. I like to look for patterns in relationships. If they lie or do something to damage the relationship once, I can give some grace. They do it twice, and I take note. They do it three times? We are going to have a conversation because now it's become a pattern. Then, I have to decide if I am willing to continue in the relationship in its current form, readjust it, or end it.

We are never obligated to stay in a relationship. We are required to love and honor, but that doesn't mean we have to be in relationship with them. This is especially true in the case of verbal, physical, or psychological abuse. We are not required to stay in any relationship in which we see these patterns—even if it's family. In my case, although he was trustworthy in that instance, there were countless others where I felt threatened and intimidated. If I did not respond or do what he thought I should, his responses were extreme, and my heart was not safe in his care.

If I did not respond or do what he thought I should, his responses were extreme, and my heart was not safe in his care.

....

NOT ONE-SIZE-FITS-ALL
Just because you trust them doesn't mean others should, and just because someone else trusts a person doesn't mean you should. It may be helpful to your decision, but don't take that as your only indicator. Why? Because the nature of your relationship with them

is going to be different than their relationship with others. People are going to interact differently based on the dynamics—length, position, types of personality—of the relationship.

One example is when you give references or recommendation letters for people. There is an assumption that just because you know the person asking for the reference that you are going to refer or recommend them. It's also a gamble, meaning that just because they may be a great friend, it doesn't mean they will be a great employee for the particular position or culture of the potential organization.

When I get a recommendation for a potential employee it is only one part of the decision-making process. When I recommend or refer, I share my experience with the person openly and honestly. It is up to the hiring organization to do their due diligence in making sure the potential employee is the best fit. It's not on my shoulders if they do or do not get the position. I'm simply sharing my experience.

NOT SET IN STONE

Past behavior is an indicator of future behavior, but it's not 100 percent because people can change for the better or for the worse. If it's for the worse and they break your trust, you can walk in forgiveness. You can decide to forgive them for what they did in the past. We have hope that they will be different in the future. You don't have to continue this relationship in the *same way* whether they change or not. Similarly, if they are trustworthy today, that doesn't mean they will remain that way. You have heard stories of the faithful husband of thirty years who ended up being unfaithful to his wife and family or the employee that worked for the company faithfully for fifteen years who decided to embezzle funds and ended up in prison. Past behavior is an indicator, not the rule of law.

Past behavior is an indicator of future behavior, but it's not 100 percent because people can change for the better or for the worse.

....

NOT FOR THE FAINT OF HEART

When you have a deep need for the relationship, you are more vulnerable to deception. You want it to work so badly. You are infatuated and even dazzled with some of the characteristics of the person or potential outcomes of the business venture. You think of all the mutual benefits the relationship will bring, so you tend to envision the future results wearing rose-colored glasses. Oxytocin is raging, and you easily overlook red flags. This is true in every type of relationship, from business to romance. Make sure you look at all sides of the potential relationship. Don't rush it. Don't hire, date, or enter into a contract or covenant too quickly. Emotions are not great decision-makers; they are only indicators. Don't let your emotions carry you away.

NOT ABOVE THE HOLY SPIRIT

In terms of business relationships, sometimes quick decisions have to be made and proactive risk assessment is necessary. The main indicator relied upon is usually the past success of the company, the stock, or the person. However, as a follower of Christ you have a superpower! That's right. You have the Holy Spirit inside of you guiding you into all truth. I have heard so many stories of God leading people to sell property right before a real estate bubble burst, to invest in a certain stock, to avoid a business relationship, or sometimes to reconsider an offer they had forgotten about.

NOT UP CLOSE AND PERSONAL

Sometimes you are too close and in too deep to see clearly. The closer you are to a situation, the harder it is to see the bigger picture and put all the clues together. You have to get some distance to get clarity. I just heard of a friend's daughter who lived in an apartment complex that kept having fires break out. The last time one broke out it was directly above her in a unit that was recently vacant. Imagine her shock when she found out a friend of hers was setting the fires. She kept wondering why her "friend" did not alert her. My friend's daughter was the last one out of the building, and her "friend" did not even call. She thought maybe she was in shock or just distracted. No one would ever have suspected the person. She took care of children for a living, and she had eaten dinner with this person. They spent enough time together to consider them a friend. They were similar in age, and both had daughters the same ages. We have a tendency to view those most like us to be trustworthy if we are trustworthy. She was frightened and confused when the person was arrested. She and her daughter were just too close to see the signs but not close enough to see the person's heart.

When detectives are looking for evidence against someone, they don't have to get too close; they just follow from a distance and watch the trail the person leaves. Where they spend their time, their profession, their hobbies and their money show what they value, and the people they talk to along that trail give them all the information they need. I am not suggesting we hire a private investigator for all our relationships—although I have thought about it! But we need perspective if we are going to be in close relationships with people. That's why I love the gift of community. When you are in community, everyone gets perspective on the relationships developed there, and there's a little more safety.

When detectives are looking for evidence against someone,
they don't have to get too close; they just follow from
a distance and watch the trail the person leaves.

....

NOT FOR THE SHALLOW

When someone can't admit fault or be vulnerable with you, a deep relationship is highly unlikely. You may be tempted to be vulnerable

with them because you realize that is a doorway to deeper relationships. You may attempt to be vulnerable in hopes that they will
be open with you, but if they do not reciprocate, you are setting
yourself up for them to use what you say against you at a later time.

We had a friend who continued to tell us that everything was
wonderful and positive whenever we talked. We did so many things
together, yet, inside, my gut kept loudly telling me not to trust this
person. All outward appearances seemed shiny, but a few things
stood out. They were sarcastic, and some of their comments were
dark—even sinister and judgmental in a negative way. I never heard
this person apologize or take responsibility for any pain they caused
or mistakes they made. In fact, I never even heard them tell a story
about or mention any weakness they had. If any issue arose, they
were quick to blame others and seemed obsessed with appearing
successful. It seemed that they were an expert at everything.

Other people came to them for advice and leadership, but we soon
learned they didn't have any deep relationships. Everything was
surface. As our relationship with them continued, it seemed like
they became less and less genuine. One day, thoughts that they had
about us but had never expressed to us personally began to show
up online on their social media. They were not calling our name.
It was more passive-aggressive in nature, but we knew and others
could tell that their comments were referring to us.

My suspicions were later confirmed. Someone who never had the courage to talk to us truthfully decided instead to talk about us publicly and allow others to join in on the slander on a social platform. I lost all respect for them. The values they espoused did not line up with their behavior. I should have seen the signs. They became very judgmental of the heart motivations of others, yet they never spoke of the condition of their own heart.

RULES OF THUMB

1) Betrayal affects everyone close to a relationship. No one gets out unscathed.

2) There is always collateral damage: children in a failed marriage, victims of war, parents of the child who got their heart broken, etc.

3) Betrayal has more to do with what is going inside the betrayer—their desires, fears, and dreams—than it has to do with you.

4) "Trust, but verify," is a quote from former president Ronald Reagan. You can trust people but also hold them accountable.

5) You are more trusting when you are more trustworthy. Suspicious people's behavior often mirrors their own hearts. They know what they are capable of, so they suspect you may do as they would do.

6) You do not have to join the court of public opinion.

One thing I'll never understand is the harsh judgments people render toward one another knowing we all have a propensity to get things wrong. Everyone wants grace, but few give genuine grace. Instead, we look to name-calling and shouting opinions and snarky and sarcastic comments from the rooftops of social media.

Everyone wants grace, but few give it.

This week alone, the news reported a well-known pastor was accused of inappropriate behavior, and on national television, Will Smith slapped a fellow actor/comedian. So much debate arose! Staged or not, the court of public opinion was in session on both accounts! Everyone let everyone else know who was right and who was wrong. Using words like "disgrace," "a stain," "disgusting." Every time someone fails, the crowd shouts, "Let the crucifixion begin!" It may be a literal one considering commentary, chatter, fines, sanctions, and cancel culture.

Why do people make such harsh comments? Are we afraid that if we don't judge that everyone will think it's acceptable? Who made us the judge and jury? It sounds so prideful. We have no idea what we would do with the same set of circumstances. Do we not see these people have kids, families, parents, and people who love them that are hurt by the vitriol? Do we not see that they are fellow human beings prone to making mistakes? Are we really that shocked or flawless? Have we made mistakes? Do we want our mistakes entered into the court of public opinion?

My belief is we all have an inner critic letting us know when we miss the mark, and if we are a Christian, we have the Holy Spirit to show us—in a loving way—how to change. In other words, most people are beating themselves up. They don't need our judgments. They already feel bad enough. You don't have to judge others! Let's be merciful to one another and not chime in with the crowd. Maybe we could consider extending an encouraging word, an act of kindness, and go against the flow with blessing instead of cursing. Judgment rarely changes anything, yet mercy changes everything. Think of a time you were shown mercy when you didn't deserve it. Didn't it make you want to do better? It's like someone believed in your inner goodness. Love can really change the atmosphere.

Trust is like currency. You can invest it. You can spend it. You can lose it. You can waste it. It takes time to build it—and to build it back once you've lost it. I stated earlier that trusting another person feels like giving them a piece of your heart because, essentially, you are. Understanding the complexity of trust and all its nuances will give you the ability to have an informed heart as you enter or reenter the world of deeper relationships. Let's determine to build our relationships on principles not personalities.

Chapter 8

KEEPING YOUR HEART SAFE

I got trust issues because people got lying issues.
—Unknown

*When you fully trust someone without any doubt, you finally
get one of two results: a person for life or a lesson for life.*
—Unknown

King Solomon warned his people, in Proverbs 4:23 (TLV), "Guard your heart diligently, for from it flow the springs of life." Defining expectations and values in relationships is one way you will safeguard your heart, so you have healthy trusting relationships. Other versions of the Bible interchange "diligently" with "above all else." This tells us how important it is for us to keep watch and pay attention to what gets into our heart. The only gateways into our heart are our eyes (what or whom we look at) and our ears (what or whom we listen to). What gets into our heart is what grows. Our heart is a multiplier; therefore, it will grow whatever we put into it.

Jesus even compared our heart to different types of soil in Luke 8:11-15 (NIV):

> *"This is the meaning of the parable: The seed is the word of God. Those along the path are the ones who hear, and then the devil comes and takes away the word from their hearts, so that they may not believe and be saved. Those on the rocky ground are the ones who receive the word with joy when they hear it, but they have no root. They believe for a while, but in the time of testing they fall away. The seed that fell among thorns stands for those who hear, but as they go on their way they are choked*

by life's worries, riches and pleasures, and they do not
mature. But the seed on good soil stands for those with
a noble and good heart, who hear the word, retain it,
and by persevering produce a crop."

I think we all desire to have that good soil. The one that grows in wisdom. As we endeavor to guard our hearts, it's about both what we put in and what we keep out. You have probably heard the saying "Garbage in garbage out," but the opposite is also true, "Treasure in treasure out"! Two huge barriers that need to stay out of our heart are offense and unforgiveness. They are way too heavy to carry and not meant for you to bear. As followers of Jesus, we have been forgiven much. Matthew 18 contains a powerful parable where a king forgives someone for a great debt, yet the one forgiven refuses to have mercy on someone who owes them a smaller debt. The king heard and threw the unmerciful servant into prison.

As we endeavor to guard our hearts, it's about
both what we put in and what we keep out.

. . . .

When we fully realize the massive debt of which God has forgiven us, we can't help but be merciful to those who hurt us. As freely as we have received God's forgiveness, let's give it to others. When we hold on to unforgiveness and offense, we are the ones who suffer most. Give yourself a gift by releasing the weight. Forgiveness means that people don't owe you anything. It doesn't mean what they did wasn't hurtful or wrong; it just means you trust God to deal with them. God is big enough to take care of the person who hurt you. He is your defender and healer. They are no longer your responsibility to punish or to change. Just let them go.

Letting them and it go doesn't mean you have to be in a relationship with the person who hurt you or that they can be close to you again. You can prayerfully decide that, but holding on to unforgiveness is like drinking poison and expecting the other person to die. The faster you let it go the faster you get to heal. Make room in your heart for more love. Get the negative out, put all the good treasure in your heart, and get ready to GROW!

IDENTITY
There are many experiences that can affect how we see ourselves. Our identity formation and the evolution of our identity is a complex process that causes us to have a unique view of ourselves. It is impacted by a variety of internal and external factors like society, family, loved ones, ethnicity, race, culture, location, opportunities, media, interests, appearance, self-expression, life experiences, profession, religion, gender, disabilities, and politics.

The way we see and value ourselves will significantly impact our relationships. If we have experienced significant pain or trauma, we may have certain beliefs about ourselves that leave us vulnerable to being treated poorly. If we experience rejection, then we can falsely believe that our value is diminished. If we do not see ourselves as valuable, then we may accept being treated poorly as what we deserve or the best we can hope for. We are all made in the image of God. He placed his divine nature within each and every person. Every person matters to God, and they should also matter to us.

When we realize that we are so incredibly valued and cherished and we see ourselves in that light, then we do not allow others to devalue us. No matter what we have done or how we have behaved, we do not carry any label that would cause us to have a negative view of ourselves. You were made in the image of God. You are not a mistake, you are not junk, you are not your past, and you are not what you did. You are a child of God made in His image with limitless potential. If you struggle to rid yourself of old labels, meditate on this scripture: "I praise you, for I am fearfully and won-derfully made. Wonderful are your works; my soul knows it very well" (Psalm 139:14, ESV).

We know the more you hear something, the more you will believe it. We want to believe the truth about who we are. Romans 10:17 (ESV) says this: "So faith comes from hearing, and hearing through the word of God." The Word of God says you are fearfully and won-derfully made, so repeat this out loud until your soul knows it full well. Then you will be able to discern who is worthy of giving your heart to or whom you can trust with your heart.

You can tell what is in a person's heart by the words they speak. In Matthew 12:34 (ESV), it says, "Out of the abundance of the heart the mouth speaks." When you are able to win the battle in your mind about your identity, you will know it because you will begin to speak more positively about yourself and grow in confidence. Many people cite a 2005 National Science Foundation study that asserted, "The average person thinks between twelve thousand and sixty thousand thoughts per day. Of those thousands of thoughts as many as 80% of them are negative, and 95% are exactly the same repetitive thoughts as the day before." So, there is truly a battle in your mind and heart over the truth. You have everything you need to win this battle. You are a masterpiece that is dearly loved and has great value. Your soul needs to know this full well.

You are a masterpiece that is dearly loved and has
great value. Your soul needs to know this full well.

....

VALUES AND EXPECTATIONS

It is important that we identify values and expectations and that we define the relationship or have the "DTR" talk (define the relationship). It all comes down to you deciding what your values are personally and the values and expectations you have for the relationships in your life. You must define your core values. For example, if I value hard work, honesty, communication, and physical affection in a romantic relationship, and I am dating someone who is displaying lazy tendencies, has lied to me, and is distant when we are together, it doesn't matter how good looking, sweet, or funny they are because those aren't what I value most.

One issue is that few people take the time to decide what they value. They simply settle for what comes their way. They get dazzled by a few charming characteristics. Then they are confused and upset when things don't turn out the way they had hoped. Determine what you value in the relationships in your life. What do you expect in a friend, a romantic relationship, a coworker, a boss, etc.? Once you have determined exactly what you value, write it down. Then communicate it up-front to those you are in a relationship with or are seeking a relationship with. These are nuanced conversations. I don't suggest you nail them on the door like the Reformation Theses.

Have a careful, intentional conversation where you ask them what they value and expect from you. Share your desires with them as well. Then as you discuss each other's values, it should be clear how you can move forward or if something needs to change. It should be a very enlightening conversation. You should share some of the same values, or you will live in continual conflict as situations arise.

I remember going on a date with a very handsome guy. I was so excited about that date. He took me to a really nice restaurant and things were going great. Then he ordered an alcoholic drink or two. I was unable to continue that relationship because I had already decided that was not going to be something I would engage in. I valued sobriety. I had lived a party lifestyle that led to many mistakes, and no good thing resulted from it. Once I gave my life to Christ, I knew I wanted something different. I knew I could not entertain another date with him because we did not share the same values. I saved us both future heartache by being up-front at the beginning.

Another time, I went on a blind date with a guy who came on entirely too strong. He picked me up in a fancy car, we went to a great performance, and he kept trying to hold my hand during the performance. I could not go along with pretending to like someone that I barely knew. I leaned toward the other side of the seat, and he started to pout. In my mind, it was over at that point. His immaturity was repellant. He drove me to my car, and I jumped in so fast that when he walked over to my window, leaned in, and tried to kiss me, I had to push him back. The next morning, he called me at 6 am! When I answered, he said, "Hi, sweetie—a term that it was entirely too early to use. He said he knew I got up early for church and wanted to talk before I left. I said, "Not this early!" He then proceeded to call me thirteen times that day.

I was afraid to reject him and hurt him, so I thought I could just go ghost. (I know that is worse.) Finally, I was aggravated enough to answer, and I had a revelation: *I don't have to give him a reason.* In this case, I had like one hundred reasons, but I realized I did not owe him anything. So, I just simply said, "Thank you for the date, but this just isn't going to work." He asked why, and I said that it just wasn't. He got angry, said he hoped I find what I'm looking for, and hung up. He called the next day to apologize, read me a poem he had written, and asked for another chance. I simply replied again, "No, thank you."

That date really helped me determine what I valued and what I did not. It also helped me to be more up-front and bolder with expressing myself. He was a romantic, passionate, financially secure, nice-looking guy. He smelled good. He had a nice car. All those things I valued, but I apparently valued a few other things even more: taking things slow, physical boundaries, emotional maturity and consistency, great listening skills, and the ability to read body language and pick up on social cues. Sometimes we have encounters that, even though they are unpleasant, are great learning opportunities, and they help us in the future as we set our expectations, flesh out our core values, and define our relationships. I hope it was a learning experience for him as well.

The "Define the Relationship" talk is important in every relationship—not just romantic ones.

The DTR talk is important in every relationship—not just romantic ones. Everyone needs to know what they can expect from one another so that they don't end up with unmet expectations because they were never communicated at the start. We assume expectations so many times. Each type of relationship—business, customer service, government, pastoral, or friendships—comes with its own set of expectations. We come from diverse backgrounds with different belief systems and distinct standards and ways of doing things. If we are not intentional about how we are going to operate in relationship with one another, we will end up disappointed and disillusioned. We will project our standards and desires on people who may not share the same, and we may unfairly expect something they never said they could offer and may not even be capable of. Once we define what we both need, we can decide if the relationship can proceed or not.

Expectations have two sides: the expected outcome and the reality. If people meet our expectations, we can, over time, become ungrateful. If they don't meet our expectations, we can become offended. We also have uncommunicated and/or unrealistic expectations. That is why it is so important to discuss them. In some cases, you may not know that you had an expectation until you are in the moment. That is okay; it's never too late to communicate what is important to you. One thing that helped me a lot in this area was being in community with people who were really good at stating the truth in a direct but loving way. It helped me to be stronger. I borrowed their strength. Maybe you are someone who needs strength. Maybe you are strong, and you can lend your strength to someone who struggles to stand up for what's important to them. Lend your strength by modeling it in your own relationships. You don't have to get involved in their relationships; instead, you equip them to navigate theirs.

While these are steps to help us find and deepen great relationships, they are not always going to weed out hurtful people. I also know stories about people who can act and mimic the signs of trust very well. I have met a few of them. They totally could win an Academy Award for their performances of being someone else until you are deep into the relationship, and then their dark side seems to come out of nowhere.

However, there is always a way out. Just be super clear about what you need and what you won't tolerate. What your values are, what your expectations are, and when and how you communicate them with others are important. Have the define the relationship talk. Get detailed.

» How often do you expect to communicate, and how will you do it?
» How do you expect to handle disagreements?
» What are some deal breakers?
» Who pays for what?
» What is very important to you, and what are things you don't like but aren't that big of a deal to you?

The more you communicate, the less frustrated you will be.

We must define what's most important to us in a God-centered relationship. Then, we commit to becoming the best version of ourselves for God.

DEFINE EXPECTATIONS

IN DATING:
- » How often will we talk?
- » How often will we go out?
- » How much money will we spend on one another?
- » Who pays for what?
- » What physical boundaries will we put in place to keep us from temptation?
- » How do we handle fights and arguments?
- » Is yelling acceptable?
- » Is hitting each other acceptable? (I'll answer this for you—NO!)
- » Do we do the silent treatment?
- » How should we communicate when we are angry?
- » What are our default reactions in anger, and how can we hold each other accountable for growing out of these defaults?
- » Do we share our problems with others? If so, whom?
- » What roles will we each take on when it comes to household responsibilities?

» What are the expectations we both have when it comes to raising children?

» What are our goals?

» How will our relationship help us to advance our goals?

IN BUSINESS:

» What is your role?

» What is my role?

» How will we communicate?

» Who has the final say on decisions?

» What is the budget?

» Who does what by when?

» What is our mission?

» What are our values?

» What type of culture do we want to develop?

» How do we know if we are winning or losing?

» Is everyone clear on their role in the mission and vision?

» Is everyone clear on their part in it?

» What happens if this relationship ends?

» What will we do for a succession plan?

Those are just a few questions to get you started, but make sure you consider all aspects of your relationship as you define your values and expectations.

Your heart is never safer than when it is whole. Wholeness comes when you are healing, growing, and trusting the truth.

Chapter 9

TRUSTING GOD THROUGH HARD TIMES

Never be afraid to trust an unknown future to a known God.
—Corrie Ten Boom

'Tis So Sweet to Trust in Jesus[23]

by Louisa M. R. Stead

'Tis so sweet to trust in Jesus,

Just to take Him at His Word;

Just to rest upon His promise,

And to know, "Thus saith the Lord!"

Refrain:

Jesus, Jesus, how I trust Him!

How I've proved Him o'er and o'er;

Jesus, Jesus, precious Jesus!

Oh, for grace to trust Him more!

Oh, how sweet to trust in Jesus,

Just to trust His cleansing blood;

And in simple faith to plunge me

'Neath the healing, cleansing flood!

Yes, 'tis sweet to trust in Jesus,

Just from sin and self to cease;

Just from Jesus simply taking

Life and rest, and joy and peace.

I'm so glad I learned to trust Thee,

Precious Jesus, Savior, Friend;

And I know that Thou art with me,

Wilt be with me to the end.

---

23 Louisa M. R. Stead, "'Tis so Sweet to Trust in Jesus," *Hymnary.org*, hymnary.org/text/tis_so_sweet_to_trust_in_jesus_just_to.

T his beautiful hymn was written by Louisa M. R. Stead in 1882 during a time of great pain in her life. Quoting hymnologist Kenneth Osbeck, C. Michael Hawn with the United Methodist Church's Discipleship Ministries recounted the event that would birth this hymn:

> *"When her child was four years of age, the family decided one day to enjoy the sunny beach at Long Island Sound, New York. While eating their picnic lunch, they suddenly heard cries of help and spotted a drowning boy in the sea. Mr. Stead charged into the water. As often happens, however, the struggling boy pulled his rescuer under water with him, and both drowned before the terrified eyes of wife and daughter. Out of her 'why?' struggle with God during the ensuing days glowed these meaningful words from the soul of Louisa Stead."*[24]

Trusting God does not mean that the chapters of our lives will be free from suffering or pain. It does mean that God will ultimately make meaning out of the chapters of our lives. If it's not good now, then God isn't done yet. Louisa went on to continue work as a missionary, although she suffered from a lifelong illness. She married again, and at the end of her life, having passed her faith and trust on to another generation, the people she ministered to continued to sing the hymn she wrote. Many hymns that are still sung today were birthed out of great pain. We could not begin to guess how

---

24   C. Michael Hawn, "History of Hymns: 'Tis so Sweet to Trust in Jesus,'" *Discipleship Ministries*, 17 Sept. 2014, www.umcdiscipleship.org/resources/history-of-hymns-tis-so-sweet-to-trust-in-jesus.

many great works of art, songs, sculptures, paintings, plays, movies, inventions, and creations have come as the result of pain.

Trusting God does not mean that the chapters of our lives will be free from suffering or pain. It does mean that God will ultimately make meaning out of the chapters of our lives.

Famous artist Sophie Calle wrote this regarding her body of work created for the French Pavilion of the 2007 Venice Biennale:

I received an email telling me it was over.
I didn't know how to respond.
It was almost as if it hadn't been meant for me.
It ended with the words, "Take care of yourself."
And so I did.
I asked 107 women (including two made from wood and one with feathers),
chosen for their profession or skills, to interpret this letter.
To analyze it, comment on it, dance it, sing it.
Dissect it. Exhaust it. Understand it for me.
Answer for me.
It was a way of taking the time to break up.
A way of taking care of myself.[25]

---

25 Sophie Calle, *Take Care of Yourself* (Arles, France: Actes Sud Publishing, 2007).

After reading about this fascinating artist, I did a little more research and found that this particular collection of artwork had been published as a book: *Sophie Calle: Take Care of Yourself.* I found it on Amazon! Last I checked, it was going for anywhere between $675 and $1,900 because it is a collector's item. This is how Amazon describes it:

> *In this remarkable artist's book, French conceptual artist/provocateur Sophie Calle presents 107 outside interpretations of a "breakup" email she received from her lover the day he ended their affair.... The result is a fascinating study and a deeply moving experience–as well as an artwork in its own right. Already a collector's item, this is a universal document of how it feels to grieve for love.[26]*

Sophie Calle took care of herself! She took heartbreak and turned it into artwork and therapy that would touch the hearts of countless others. I found one source that stated her net worth is around $187 million.[27] I went down a rabbit hole learning about her. I love the way she took her pain and turned it into art. She has a plethora of other works that are equally fascinating!

---

26 Sophie Calle, et al., "Sophie Calle: And so Forth," *Amazon*, Prestel, 2016, www.amazon.com/Sophie-Calle-Take-Care-Yourself/dp/2742768939/ref=sr_1_7?crid=1WODZ7GUL6EC2&keywords=sophie%2Bcalle&qid=1649727140&sprefix=sophie%2Bcalle%2Caps%2C106&sr=8-7.

27 "Sophie Calle Net Worth, Biography, Age, Weight, Height," *NetWorthRoll*, 1 Jan. 2020, networthroll.com/sophie-calle-net-worth/.

Other great works of art were birthed from relational pain:

» The Kiss (1882) and The Eternal Idol (1890–93) by Auguste Rodin were created after a volatile relationship ended.
» Frida Kahlo painted The Two Fridas (1939) and La Venadita or Little Deer (1946) after her tumultuous marriage ended in heartbreak when the husband she trusted cheated on her with her sister. She also had suffered chronic pain since childhood after a terrible accident and many of her paintings depict it.
» Ashes (1895) was created by Edvard Munch created after the dissolution of one of his tempestuous romances. It depicts his anguish, his female counterpart's triumph, and the ashes of what connected the two of them.[28]

Our greatest tests give birth to our greatest testimonies! Over the years, I have heard many stories of tragedy turned into triumph. It did not always happen immediately or exactly how they wanted it to, but it always happened. Whether it was the unexplainable death of a child, spouse, sibling, or friend, a chronic illness, the loss of a job, scholarship, or opportunity, divorce, imprisonment, addiction, heartbreak, or bankruptcy, the way God has worked in those situations has been nothing short of miraculous. While the triumph does not diminish the anguish or grief in those situations, the resounding collective response I have heard from those who have endured the pain is that God met them right in the middle of

---

28 Alexxa Gotthardt, "8 Famous Artists Who Turned Heartbreak into Art," *Artsy*, 11 Feb. 2019, www.artsy. net/article/artsy-editorial-8-famous-artists-turned-heartbreak-art.

the pain and walked them through it step by step. Many of them said it was during those times when they felt Him the most.

Our greatest tests give birth to our greatest testimonies!

....

We don't see how He makes our tragedies into something beautiful, but He is the God who does what seems impossible! Even when things aren't good, God is still good. I've heard it said that the richest growth is found in the valley, not on the mountaintop. I think that is true. Although we don't invite the seasons in the valley, they are where we grow the most.

> *And we know that for those who love God all*
> *things work together for good, for those who*
> *are called according to his purpose.*
> —Romans 8:28 (ESV)

Many people have been disappointed with God because they expected that things would go a certain way in their lives or the lives of those they love. When those expectations aren't met, they feel they can no longer trust Him. We have to remember that God is sovereign and not subject to us; rather, we are to be subject to Him. I still believe we can stand on His promises, and we can pray and come into agreement with Him, and circumstances can change. I have seen that happen. I have come to believe exactly what His Word says: He is working all things together for our good no matter what. Even when the pain is so unbearable I feel I can't live another day. Even when I don't understand what possible good could come out of it, I rest in the fact that He is bigger, wiser, all-knowing and all-present. I don't have to understand to trust Him. He has proven His faithfulness. He always will.

I don't have to understand God to trust Him.
He has proven His faithfulness.

Look at the life of a butterfly and the metamorphosis that it undergoes. It starts out in one state and transforms into another. What if a butterfly chose to judge any stage of its journey by its current circumstance?

It goes from an egg ... to a caterpillar ... to a pupa ... then a butterfly. It starts out as a very small egg. Then, as a caterpillar, it is in the feeding stage and grows to one hundred times its egg size, but its viewpoint is limited to wherever it can crawl. Then it goes into the transition phase, where its strength is built, and it gains wings, eyes, and legs. It may be hidden away during this phase.

In each stage, its perspective is limited by its current circumstance, experience, and maturity. If it could reason and speak, it might ask God, "Why have You made this so hard? Why can't I be more _____? I will always feel this way. This seems unfair! I have no special skill, talent, or beauty." Finally, one day, it pops out a beautiful, majestic butterfly. Then it all makes sense; each stage was necessary for growth. Its perspective goes as high as it can fly and as low as it can land.

We only see a small piece of the masterpiece God is making with our lives. Don't allow the limitations and heartaches in your current stage of life to make you believe that it will always feel this way. There is a whole new perspective awaiting you as you hold on to hope and learn from your experiences. You may be in a tight spot now, but you will mature, expand, and soar!

There are two sides to expectation. If I do what you expect, then you can become ungrateful. If I don't do what you expect, then you can become offended. We can look at this principle with people and even with God. When everything is going our way, we can forget to be grateful to God, but when things are going badly, we can be upset with God for allowing that to happen. We eventually learn that expectations are not absolute truths. Just because we expect things to go a certain way doesn't mean they will, and when they don't, we do not need to be so surprised. Let's keep our faith high and our praises high. God can do exceedingly abundantly more than we can ask, think, or imagine. When we are in a storm, we can only see one possible outcome. The truth is there are many possible outcomes to your situation. God sees them all and will use every bit of your story to show His faithfulness.

As Jesus' disciples were with him in a storm, they could only see one outcome—impending doom! They were with Jesus! He could have solved the issue many different ways but chose to speak to the wind and the waves. He commanded, "Peace! Be still!" in Mark 4:39 (ESV). In the storm, we may be tempted to blame, shame, run away, self-medicate, or manipulate, but the only action we need to take is to invite Jesus into our situation. When everything is loud, we need to get quiet and hear His voice speaking peace to our souls. We must keep our eyes on Him in the storm. If your life were like a huge puzzle, God would not show you the whole puzzle. Instead, He might show you one piece or a few at a time. Listen to His voice, and follow His leading.

I was so excited about life and following Jesus in my last year of college. I was growing deeper in my faith and just felt like a whole new person! I had healed from that last relationship when a new relationship entered my life. I had admired this guy from afar. He was nothing like anyone I had ever dated. He was a football player at the University of Georgia, and he was paired with me to help with college football recruit visits as part of the football recruiting process. I found out the reason we were paired was because we were both Christians, and they would give us the Christian recruits.

I was selected to be a Georgia Girl. This was a part of the recruiting program where we were assigned a potential recruit and their family to host and give a tour of the college for the day. I loved being a Georgia Girl. We got to have really great free food before the game and at halftime. We got to ride the buses behind the players and walk on the field with them at every home game. We had great seats, and I got to meet so many people. One potential recruit that I had the pleasure of hosting was Patrick Mannelly who ended up going to Duke and then on to play for the Chicago Bears. It was just so much fun to be a part of this program.

As the football player I was paired with and I spent time together communicating about the recruits, we began to develop a relationship. I adored him, and he made me laugh. He went on to play professionally for two teams, and during that time, he began to call me. We went on a few dates, and when he got injured, he ultimately came home and decided to answer the call to preach. We dated and had the best time. It was the most pure relationship I had ever had. We memorized scripture together, went on incredible dates, and loved going to church together. Our relationship was centered around Jesus, and I was in awe of how healthy—and holy—it was.

After about a year or less of dating, we got engaged. We had gone back to visit our college campus on one of our dates and it was during spring training. We walked out on the field at Sanford Stadium, between the hedges, and he totally shocked me when he got down on one knee and proposed. I felt like I was living a fairy tale. Are you kidding me? Between the hedges of Sanford Stadium, he got on one knee and gave me a beautiful diamond ring. I was floating! I was so in love and so excited for the future we would build together.

We planned a beautiful wedding. His mom, whom I adored, rode with us to pick out our first apartment on his seminary campus in South Carolina. I had picked a great place for our reception. I had my mom's wedding dress taken from storage and was having it altered to fit me. We bought our first piece of furniture. Everything was perfect. Until it wasn't. We never argued or fought, and, one time, he thought he had hurt my feelings, and he came to my window with flowers apologizing. It just did not add up. I had gone to New York to see him during his time serving a church there, and while we had a great time, I noticed that he kept trying to pull something out of me like he was trying to make me into someone that I wasn't. He wanted me to be more outgoing which is funny because I actually am. Looking back, I never could really be myself with him because I idolized him, and this very God-centered way of living was all so new to me. I was afraid I would mess it up, so I never was really me.

One afternoon, I was preparing to go to a dress fitting and had just returned from our reception venue when he called. I had a friend over, and he asked me to request that she leave which was odd. I did what he requested, and he told me he didn't think he could marry me. He just didn't have peace anymore. I was not outgoing enough, and I wasn't pastor's wife material. All I kept hearing was that *I wasn't enough*. I was devastated—shocked, bewildered, and gutted! My pain was unbearable. I screamed, I cried, and I jumped in my car and headed to my small group leader's house. She called some of the ladies, and they came over at once and prayed with me. While they were just as bewildered as I was, I'll never forget how well they loved me through it all.

All I kept hearing was that I wasn't enough.

....

What was interesting was that we had been going through a Bible study on the book of Job with the theme "Gaining through Losing." We went around to each person and asked, "What do you want to get out of this study?" It became clear everyone was scared that God would teach them something about loss as we went through this study, and He might take something from us. None of us wanted to lose anything. I remember thinking, *God, please don't take this from me!* when we started the study. I didn't even want to utter it out loud. Why did I fear that? I think I was wrestling with the questions: *Can I really trust God to bring good into my life? Do I deserve good?*

In the end, he flew home, and we went driving around while I cried, and he talked. I played over in my mind him saying, "I just don't think you are pastor's wife material." That stung. I never wanted to be a pastor's wife in the first place. I just wanted to be his wife. I actually wanted to be a missionary in a foreign country. Whatever his idea about what a pastor's wife was supposed to be, I wasn't it. More rejection heaped up. He was unfamiliar with the particular area I lived in but was more familiar with a town about forty-five minutes away, so we went there, and I covered those streets with my tears. I had only been there with him twice before, so I wasn't as familiar with it as he was. At one point, I cried so hard he pulled over by a white picket fence. I now live in that town, and our church (the one God allowed Michael and me to plant) is on the same road that I watered with my tears. I couldn't see it then, but God was going to restore everything and give me more than I could have dreamed of. I thought my life was over, but it had only just begun.

I spent the next few weeks in a daze, battling thoughts of taking my life. I couldn't eat or sleep—which had never been an issue for me before. My sweet parents had worked so hard to save and put me through college with no debt. They had not taken a vacation in years. It just so happened that our broken engagement was just before my first wedding shower and right before our first family vacation in years. Needless to say, it was a miserable vacation for everyone because I was so distraught and filled with despair. I believed that this rejection was not only from my fiancé but from God. It was as if God had dangled this beautiful relationship in front of me and cruelly snatched it away showing me that I wasn't worthy of it. I felt rejected by God.

It was as if God had dangled this beautiful relationship in front of me and cruelly snatched it away showing me that I wasn't worthy of it. I felt rejected by God.

....

I planned to take my life when we returned home. I was going to wait until my parents were asleep and take every pill I could find in the cabinet. Instead, I fell into a deep sleep. I guess a week of no sleep caught up with me. That next morning, I woke up with that same stabbing stomach pain that seemed to say, *This is your reality. This is not a nightmare you can wake up from.* I was broken and humiliated. I would have to explain this to everyone. His mom had to explain it at my wedding shower because it was too late to cancel it. I had to tell all my friends, coworkers, and family members. After I realized my plan to end my life had failed that night, I woke up and called him. I asked him what we were doing moving forward. I knew we weren't getting married right then, but did that mean we were breaking up or trying to give it more time?

For the first time, he was stern in his tone toward me. He said, "I guess if you have to know right now, we are breaking up." The way his tone felt so cold helped me to say, "Okay, that's all I needed to know." We ended the conversation, and we have never spoken again. That was about twenty-eight years ago. It turns out that the person I thought I couldn't live without ... I could, and I have. I walked into my home's family room, and my best friend had shown up at my house because she was so worried about me. She said, "You look different." I replied, "I think I'm going to be okay." I can't explain it. A peace had washed over me. I had closure. He came over, and I gave his ring back to him.

I took the next four years and poured my life into serving God. I heard Joyce Meyer once say that if you are hurting, get your eyes off of yourself, and put them on someone else who is hurting. Serve them.

Scripture teaches us that those who water others will themselves be watered. I did just that. I went on mission trips, served as a chaperone to anyone who needed help, and ministered at multiple churches' vacation Bible school events. I went to Russia on a fourteen-day trip sharing the gospel. It was amazing. I participated in Bible studies and memorized scriptures that carry me to this day. I couldn't believe how quickly my heart began to heal.

I also had to get unforgiveness out of my heart. I'd had all these feelings bottled up in my heart. So one day I wrote him a ten-page letter. I wrote everything I was feeling. I described how badly he had hurt me. That letter was filled with love but also anger, resentment, anguish, and sarcasm. I wept while I wrote it. I never sent it, though. In fact, I still have it, tucked in a drawer. I just knew I had to get all of those feelings out of my heart. Only then would I be able to release it and let it all go. Something about getting those feelings onto paper healed something in me.

I decided that, in order to keep my heart safe, I was to be married to Jesus and even wore a ring. His Word said He would NEVER leave me or forsake me, so I would stick with Him. When my friend began telling me about my now husband, Michael, I blew her off for two years. By the time I met him, four years had passed since the time of my broken heart. I finally agreed to talk to him. I had told the Lord in a prayer four years earlier that I fully trusted Him, and if He wanted me to have a husband, then He would literally have to bring him to me. I gave God my wish list, and I added, "You will have to bring him to me—literally." I refused to pursue a relationship or let anyone know that I liked them. I didn't want to have anything to do with this process. I wanted to have zero control. I wanted to know that my husband was from God 100 percent!

When I agreed to go on a blind date with Michael, I was trepidatious. He was very different—in almost every way—from anyone I had ever dated. He was serious and intense. He cared about scents, and he smelled really good! Most of all, He loved Jesus, and he was very patient and kind to me. He introduced me to anointed worship music. He could see how hesitant I was and the many walls of protection I had built up. I tried to break up with him twice, and he just kept proving to me that he was better than I ever thought possible.

We were recently interviewed about our love story. You can find the story of our blind date on YouTube (Turning Point Church, McDonough, Georgia—"Pastor Michael and Charla Love Story"[29]) as well as what followed ("The Truth About Marriage—Pastor Michael and Charla"[30]). I credit it all to God because He writes the best love stories! He led us to each other, and He sustains us. Michael was able to break down the walls I had built up. He checked every box on my wish list, and I'm so glad that God saved the best for last. We have been married for twenty-five years, and it gets better every year. We have three beautiful children, and while there have been many storms, we have had the honor of weathering them through faith together.

With Michael, God checked every box on my wish list,
and I'm so glad that He saved the best for last.

. . . .

---

29 Michael and Charla Turner, "Pastor Michael and Charla Love Story," Turning Point Church, streamed March 2022, YouTube video, 40:29, https://www.youtube.com/watch?v=TMJlLTSlv-M.

30 Michael and Charla Turner, "The Truth About Marriage—Pastor Michael and Charla," Turning Point Church, streamed April 2022, 51:05, https://www.youtube.com/watch?v=QkicWHyAWzs&t=127s.

We had a miscarriage before our first son was born, and that threw us both to our knees. The old wounds threatened to split open again, and the lie that I would never have kids because of my past tried to spring up, but we made a decision to stand in faith and believe: No matter what, God is good. He could be trusted. And, whatever He wanted for us would be His best. He was not punishing us. After all, we were new creations in Him. We went away to a beautiful place on a lake called Still Waters. We prayed, cried, and grieved. Then, we placed our sights on the future. We stood on the promises of God, and we meditated on them. Romans 10:17 (NKJV) says, "Faith *comes* by hearing and hearing by the word of God." The more you meditate on that promise the more your faith comes into alignment with God's will.

Some of the promises I have stood on are:

> *Children are a Heritage From the LORD. . . . Like arrows in*
> *the hand of a warrior, so are children born in one's youth.*
> *Blessed is the man whose quiver is full of them. He will not*
> *be put to shame when he confronts the enemies at the gate.*
> ——Psalm 127:3-5 (BSB)

We would say this one over and over after our miscarriage and when we were believing for a baby.

> *Delight yourself in the LORD, and he will*
> *give you the desires of your heart.*
> — Psalm 37:4 (ESV)

When I desired a husband, I would meditate on this. I would ask God to either remove the desire or help me trust Him to fulfill it.

> *And after you have suffered a little while, the God of all*
> *grace, who has called you to his eternal glory in Christ, will*
> *himself restore, confirm, strengthen, and establish you.*
> —1 Peter 5:10 (ESV)

When I couldn't stop the pain I was feeling in a particular season, I meditated on this.

Whenever we are hurt, we should always take time to grieve what *was,* but we can't stay there. We don't want a season of grief to turn into a lifetime. That is not to say we will never feel the sting or pain of heartache as we will have a measure of that until we go on to eternity, but it changes form, frequency, duration, and heaviness. We must lift our eyes to Him and to the future He has prepared for us.

My husband always says, "Instead of asking *why* ask *what*?" What can I learn? What do I do next? Our lives are like a beautiful novel. Turn the page, and get ready for the next chapter. When you experience a setback, get ready for the comeback. In Jesus, the best is always yet to come. What if I had gone through with my plans of taking my life because I could not see past that season of deep pain? I would have missed the best parts of my life! When I look at the very hard times some of my friends and church members have been through, I am so encouraged when I see that what seemed like it was going to take them out actually takes them up to a new level of faith instead. What the enemy meant for evil God used for good in their lives. If you are in a season of pain, grief, rejection, shame, or loss, stick around, and stick with God. He is faithful and trustworthy.

Nehemiah 8:10 (ESV) says, "The joy of the LORD is [my] strength." I have always looked at that scripture to mean that as I focus on the Lord my joy would come from Him, and that would be my strength. I heard another interpretation that flipped it around to mean God's joy is when I am strong! I love both thoughts.

One of the greatest secrets in trusting
God in hard times is this: Stay.

....

One of the greatest secrets in trusting God in hard times is this: STAY. Don't run away when things don't go as you think they should. If you will be faithful to your faith in Him and just stay close to Him, you will see His goodness, and you will find the healing you have been searching for.

>   **S**—*Stick close and don't let go. Stand on His promises.*
>   *(Find a scripture/promise to meditate on that deals with*
>   *the storm you are going through.)*

T—*Tell Him all your fears, doubts, and hurts as well as the things you are grateful for even if it's just the fact that you can breathe air.*

A—*Ask others how you can serve their needs, and allow God to turn your mess into a message. (What can you create or do that could bring glory to God while you are hurting? Start an organization or join one that is specific to your pain. Create a piece of artwork, write a song or a book, or build something that will help or inspire others. Ask God to show you how to heal.)*

Y—*Yield to God's will.*

Chapter 10

MOVING FORWARD AFTER BETRAYAL AND TRUSTING AGAIN

Have enough courage to trust love one more time and always one more time.

—Maya Angelou

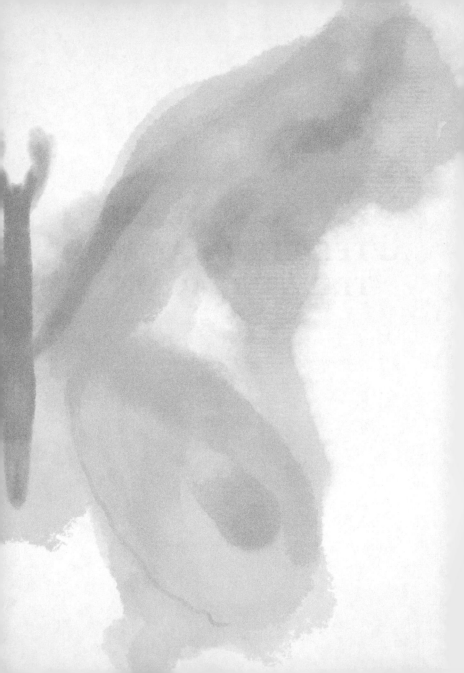

T hat day in the counselor's office was a major turning point for me. I had been in a six-year relationship that had become toxic and unbearable. I had met him on my high school senior trip. We were at the beach on the deck of a bar. (Why they let teenagers into this outdoor bar I'll never know!) He was singing along to a pretty racy song, but he was laughing, and something about the way he was dancing and the twinkle in his eye got me smitten. We played minigolf and hung out a few more times on the trip. Then, when we got home, he came over to my friend's house. He tried to have sex with me, but I refused. That should have been my first clue. I had to tell him multiple times, but he just kept trying anyway.

I was a church girl—raised to go every Sunday morning, Sunday night, and Wednesday night. I loved Jesus, I knew sex was reserved for marriage, and I wanted God's best. I had made poor choices already, and I didn't want to continue. I wasn't making all the right choices, but that one thing was something I really wanted to honor. Although my behaviors (drinking and drug use) did not line up with my values, I knew that they would one day. In my heart, I knew that I simply wanted to be loved … to be wanted. If the crowd required that lifestyle, then I was willing to compromise my values temporarily so that I could enjoy the relationships.

*In my heart, I knew that I simply wanted
to be loved … to be wanted.*

When I look back, it was always about having fun with friends.
The alcohol and drugs, in my case, were just supporting actors. I
always thought, *When I'm older, of course, I won't do this. I'll wait
to be boring when I'm older.* Wow! What a lie the enemy had me
believing. Being devoted to and living for Jesus is far from boring,
and a big plus is that I don't wake up with tons of regret. I had
to redefine fun!

So, that guy and I had a six-year relationship filled with many good
times and many really bad times. I eventually gave in to the sexual
relationship. I would cry and tell him how guilty I felt and how I
really did not want to, but he would say that I could not make that
decision for both of us because that was not fair. However, he didn't
see that by making the opposite decision for us both, he was also
being unfair. The minute we started down that path, I started to
experience emotions I had never felt before—jealousy, anger, dis-
illusionment—things that I think God wanted to protect me from.

What I saw as rules meant to keep me from having fun were actually
guardrails giving me direction that would keep me and my heart
safe and protected. My emotions had me barreling full steam ahead

in that destructive relationship. I knew that he was cheating on me, but I could never prove it. We went to two different colleges which he made sure of. I was once going to transfer into his college, but he told me the day I was to move into an apartment with friends that he would break up with me if I did. He said it was because I would expect more time than he could give, but deep down, I knew. There were several clues one of which was a girl's earring on his bed that he explained away as his roommate's girlfriend's. She verified the story, but deep inside, I knew she was lying. I just didn't want to believe it.

What I saw as rules meant to keep me from having fun were actually guardrails giving me direction that would keep me and my heart safe and protected.

The worst and most humiliating moment was when I was at his fraternity formal. I was a nervous wreck not knowing what to wear. The first year we dated, I felt like I had to learn to dress completely differently. The girls in college had a whole other style of fashion than my high school hometown. I had spent weeks looking for a dress to wear to his formal, and I didn't have any sorority girls as friends at the time. He was a year ahead of me, and I hadn't started college yet.

I felt like I was learning everything on my own as I went. I learned a lot and made a lot of mistakes, but by the time his senior year formal came around, I was a seasoned pro at what to wear. This particular year, he decided to skip the "senior burn run through" that was an important tradition. He stopped by and told them he wanted to spend extra time with me, so he wasn't participating, and he warned them not to do anything that would hurt me.

I don't know why they chose me as the object of their horrible tradition, but they did. The fraternity brothers all had their suits and Ray-Bans on. The seniors chosen to be on stage walked up like bodyguards carrying one guy on a type of plank, mat, or chair from my recollection. The details are fuzzy as it's a story I try to forget. The guy being carried was seated cross-legged with a turban on his head. They were reenacting an old bit from the Johnny Carson comedy bit "Carnac the Magnificent." Johnny would hold an envelope with a question inside to his turban. He would act like he could predict the answer: "The answer to this question is … " (insert drum roll). Then he would say the answer. After that, he would read the question, and it would be funny.

In this case, it was just mean. The fraternity brother held the envelope to his turban, and he said something like, "Mika lika high mika high me down … the answer to this question is *Ken Brown*." (The name has been changed to protect him.) Then, these words came out in a slow dramatic motion: "Who is the only *fraternity name* to take his girlfriend's pictures down during the week?" Everyone let out a deep, low sigh as if to say, "Ohhhhh!" Next, they all looked at me. I got up, ran to a bathroom stall, and cried my eyes out. His roommates came into the girls' bathroom. Girls I didn't know came in apologizing and pleading his case saying, " He loves you. I know he does." None of this helped. I just wanted to disappear. I wanted the earth to open up and swallow me whole.

The following week my boyfriend attacked the guy responsible and broke his nose. You see, I really do believe he loved me—the best way he knew how. He also wanted to play the field. The relationship began to deteriorate when he started to belittle me and call me names when I didn't do the things he wanted me to. Little things began to cause big fights. I once ate off his plate, and he got so angry. His friends were all at the table, noticed how petty he was acting, and picked at him about it. When we got to the car, he grabbed me by the face, slammed my head against the window, and called me a b-word. I began to feel like I was always apologizing for something, begging him to be with me, let me come along, or stay with me when he just wanted to be free.

There were multiple times he grew irate when I didn't follow his instructions. Once, we were on our way to a beach trip. We were almost there when we happened upon a wreck. He told me to stay in the car which I did not do. When we both got back into the car, he started yelling at me. He made a U-turn saying we were going back, and I could just go home. I was devastated. Adventures and beach trips were the most exciting thing in my life, and I had been looking forward to this trip for a long time. I began to think I should have listened to him and just obeyed? (Wait … what? Why do I need to obey him?) I blamed myself. He eventually cooled down, and we went on the trip. Another time, he threw me up against a wall because I begged him to stay with me, and I called him out on the real reason he was leaving me to go to this particular event. He wanted to look good in front of this certain family by showing up at their church. I knew it was true because he never wanted to go to church. That incensed him, and I regretted my comment.

The names he called me were ugly and damaged my self-esteem. My friends hated him. Because they hated the way he treated me, my roommates once hid the phones in our apartment, so I wouldn't talk to him. No one in my life thought he was right for me. I am sharing this with you because I want you to see how desperate I was chasing after someone who wasn't able to be trusted with my heart. He wanted the relationship and the benefits of it for himself, but he was unable to give what I needed. Once I took the emotional dive and was so invested in the relationship, he probably could have beat me on the head with a hot frying pan. I would have begged him to stay and convinced myself that every mean thing he said about me was true.

Ground zero of this slippery slope toward the end of the relationship was when I got pregnant. I had been trying to bring my parents into the conversation. I deeply loved them, and they deeply loved me. I knew their expectations and desires would be against birth control, but I tried to just test the waters by asking if I could get on birth control because I had heard it helped to regulate a woman's cycle. They immediately saw through my request. They blew up. My dad said, "If I find out you are having sex, you are coming home from college!"

My dad wasn't a bad guy; he just wanted to protect me. Throughout his whole life, there were whispers about who his dad really was. My grandmother, I learned later in my life, had left her first husband for my grandfather, and my dad was a product of that relationship before they were married. Everything was very secretive and hush, hush back in those days—especially so with my family. Those whispers must have caused a deep sense of shame. After my grandmother died, my dad opened a letter from her that read: "Your father is your father." My dad wept. All his life, his identity was unsure. This moment gave him something he longed for.

My parents had a good reputation, and they were literally amazing. They were just plain good people. I think my dad wanted to protect me from a pregnancy outside of marriage because he never wanted me to be judged . . . to walk in that shame. After the big blow-up, I knew I could not talk to my parents about this part of my life. When we went to the health clinic and got the positive pregnancy test, we both felt that abortion was the only option. He had big dreams and high hopes of being a successful public figure. I didn't want to be the talk of the town. I didn't want my parents or me to be judged by church people. Both are selfish reasons; I just didn't see any other way forward.

We looked up the abortion clinic in the yellow pages, called and made the appointment, and showed up—two young, barely-into-our-twenties kids with no one to talk to about this life-altering decision. We sat in the waiting room filled with regret and shame. I had prayed the night before for God to just make it not be true. I didn't want to do this. I think if my boyfriend had just said, "Let's get married and raise this baby," I would have jumped at that chance, but it was not to be. I was called into the "counselor's" office, she asked me why I wanted to go through with this, and I said, "My parents will be so ashamed of me. I just can't do this to them." She replied, "They probably won't kill you. And, they will work through this should you decide to talk to them." She didn't try very hard to dissuade me.

The next room I entered was a changing room. I donned a hospital gown on and went into a small room filled with about six other girls who were in the exact same position as I was. In any other setting, we probably would have been talking and connecting, but the shame in this room was heavy. It was like a blanket of thick grey fog—that we all wished we could hide under—covered us. Every girl looked down at her feet, not making eye contact and not saying a single word. Shame, regret, remorse, and guilt were ruling my soul, and I felt like the enemy was jamming an ice pick into my heart with every step I took closer to the procedure room. They gave us all a pregnancy test to verify that we were indeed pregnant. Then we filed out individually to the ultrasound room. In this room, a petite older nurse with blond, short hair and a German accent performed the ultrasound.

I had prayed that this was all a mistake, so when she said, "I can't find a baby," hope rose in my heart. I looked behind me where they had strategically placed the monitor, so I wouldn't be able to see it. However, at the very moment I looked, I saw a little outline and heard the words spill out of her mouth: "There it is." *It?* I quickly turned my head forward, closed my eyes tight, and repeated the lie that I had chosen to embrace. "It's not a baby. It's not a baby ... yet." In my heart, I knew it wasn't true. If it weren't a baby yet, then why did this all feel so wrong, so very wrong? I was too far in now to walk away, or so I thought. There is a scripture that I cling to now that I wish I had known then: "No temptation has seized you except what is common to man. And God is faithful; He will not let you be tempted beyond what you can bear. But when you are tempted, He will also provide an escape, so that you can stand up under it" (1 Corinthians 10:13, BSB).

There is always a way of escape. It's always easier to find the escape early in the decision-making process or, better yet, before you are in a position to have to make a decision.

There is *always* a way of escape. It's always easier to find the escape early in the decision-making process or, better yet, before you are in a position to have to make a decision. It's better to prepare than repair. For example, if I know that sexual sin is a temptation for me, then I would need to decide ahead of time what boundaries I should put in place to help uphold my values. I would make it a point to never be alone with a guy or in any position that would encourage me to fail. I would stay around groups of people, agree together on boundaries, and have an accountability partner. None of these are guarantees, but the more safety measures I put in place, the better chance I would have of upholding my values. I could have walked out of that place and said no, but the lies I believed held me there. The fear of shame held me there.

The last thing I remember is the oxygen mask going over my face. I woke up in a recovery room where they gave me juice and cookies until I was strong enough to leave. I left that day with a big bag of medicine and an even bigger broken heart. I thought some sense of relief would follow after it was over, but that relief never came. It was far from over. I went to my college apartment for the weekend where my boyfriend took good care of me and was truly worried that we had made a bad decision. However, he and I made a pact that we would never tell anyone. It was our secret forever. He had big dreams and plans, and this would be a hindrance to his reputation and mine.

I had no idea what the weight of what we had done would do to me. I believed that, because I knew what I was doing was wrong, and I did it anyway, I had signed my death certificate to hell. There was no grace left for me. God was finished with me, and I had no hope. I carried this awful secret, the weight of the sin, the regret, the shame, the fear, and the dread, and I was miserable. A few weeks went by, and I was attending a wedding shower with my best friend. When we left that day, she said, "Charla, what is wrong with you? You are not yourself. You are a different person." I burst into tears, she pulled the car into a little church parking lot, and I could not hold on to that secret any longer. That awful secret—the worst thing anyone could ever do—that horrendous, heinous, selfish act that I had done was about to lose its power over me.

I told her that she probably would not want to be my friend anymore once I told her what I had done. She assured me that would not be true. I began to share the details like a twisted and tangled ball of yarn coming unraveled until there was nothing left to say. Thankfully, she knew the perfect counselor and suggested we go see him. She even went with me.

That meeting changed my life forever. I kept thinking that if I knew God didn't want this relationship to continue, then I could let it go. Couldn't someone just tell me this is not God's will for my life? The signs should have been obvious: the beach trip fiasco, the fraternity formal, the multiple times I had clear evidence he was cheating, but I just couldn't prove it, the angry fights, the jealousy, control, and manipulation, and the time he called me a b-word and slammed my head up against the window of the car because I took a bite off his plate, and his friends teased him about his stinginess. The time he threw me against the wall because I was begging him to stay. The time I found a girl's baby picture in an Easter card that said she would miss him over Spring Break. It couldn't have been more clear, but I was blinded by emotional ties.

On the way to the counselor, that country song came on the radio. I had never heard it before, and I've never heard it since, but I felt that God was literally singing that song straight to me.

> *And after the earthquake there was a fire, but*
> *the Lord was not in the fire. And after the fire*
> *there was the sound of a gentle whisper.*
> —1 Kings 19:12 (NLT)

God speaks to us in various ways. Through the still, small voice (which is my favorite of all), circumstances, the Bible, other people, wise counselors, dreams, visions, thoughts, natural phenomena, and supernatural manifestations. I mean, if God could speak through a donkey, then I believe He could speak through a country song and even through me.

I mean, if God could speak through a donkey, then I believe He
could speak through a country song and even through me.

I arrived at the counselor's office not really knowing what to expect. I just knew that whatever I was carrying had to be laid down. I prayed for God to speak to me through this counselor. His office was in his home, and the moment I stepped in the door, I felt a sense of peace. There are homes you step into, and you can feel tension, chaos, and heaviness. Then, you step into others, and you feel joy, peace, and relief. He introduced me to his family, and then we went into his office. His voice was kind and calm and filled with grace. He began to ask me questions, and as I opened my mouth, a flood of words tumbled out dressed up in a range of emotions: anger, disappointment, sadness, fear, and pain. I told him story after story about this relationship that I was unsure of. I loved that boyfriend so much it hurt. I just wasn't sure he could love me in a way that wouldn't hurt me, and I wondered if I could learn to live that way.

He assured me that, indeed, this relationship was—without a doubt—NOT what God wanted for my life. He gave me an exercise to take home and complete. It was pertaining to soul ties. He explained that when you have sex with someone, you create what is called a soul tie to that person. People were meant to become one flesh inside the covenant of marriage, and one part of becoming one with your spouse was sex. When you have sex and are not married, you become connected or tied to that person in your soul. A spiritual, emotional connection happens. He explained that I needed to cut this tie. It sounded a little spooky—spiritual at first, but the counselor began explaining that all I really needed to do was write down everything that my boyfriend had ever done or said to me that had hurt me. Then, after each, I was to say, "I forgive you for _____." Once I had gone through the forgiveness exercise, the final step was just to say out loud with faith, "I renounce this relationship in the name of Jesus." It sounded simple enough, and I was willing to try it when I got home.

Then it was time to talk about the deep, dark, ugly secret. My hands shook, my lip quivered, I even felt the skin on my face twitch as I revealed the awful truth that I had had an abortion. This church girl who knew better had committed the unforgivable sin of murder. Flashes and images of all that had occurred popped into my mind, and I shook with shame. He very calmly looked me in the eyes, and with his beautiful Indian accent and calm, peaceful voice filled with grace, he said, "There is nothing you can do to make God stop loving you. He has already forgiven you. All you need to do is receive His forgiveness." How do you receive forgiveness? All I knew how to do was receive rejection, abuse, and insecurity. I just took what was handed to me.

How do you receive forgiveness? All I knew how
to do was receive rejection, abuse, and insecurity.
I just took what was handed to me.

He explained that all I needed to do was take God's gift of mercy—His gift of grace—and receive His forgiveness. He then looked at me and asked, "Where is the most peaceful, safe place you can think of?" He asked me to imagine myself there. I imagined my backyard. The place I grew up. The last place I still remained innocent. Then, he asked me to imagine what my baby looked like. Was the baby a boy or a girl? What color eyes did the baby have? I imagined a little boy with curly blond hair and blue eyes. He asked me to tell my baby what I was feeling. I imagined looking into his beautiful little eyes, and out loud I said, "I am so sorry. I am so very sorry. I am sorry that I chose to take your life. I never even gave you a chance. I am so sorry. I love you, and I will see you again one day in heaven. I will hold you and hug you there."

Then he had me imagine Jesus and every detail about Him. He said, "What do you want to say to Jesus?" I began to confess everything that I had done and repent to Him out loud. I pictured myself placing the baby in His strong arms, and I told Him I knew that He would take care of him until I saw him again. The counselor left the room and let me process it all and just cry. I lay on the floor and cried every tear I had. The overwhelming waves of grief rolled over and over me, and I realized all at once what I had lost. Then, what I can only explain was the peace of God came over me, and I received this love that I knew I did not deserve. I received His love and forgiveness.

I went home that day and did the exercise of breaking the soul
tie as the counselor had instructed me to do. I don't know what I
expected to happen. *After all, it's just words*, I thought to myself,
but I would soon learn the power of those faith-filled words. I
sincerely wanted this deep union with God. I'd gotten a taste, and
it was better than anything. I understood the words of Psalm 34:8
(NIV): "Taste and see that the LORD is good!" I wanted to rid myself
of anything that could come between me and God. I had to forgive
myself, and I had to forgive my boyfriend and let him go. I am not
exaggerating when I say that, within five minutes of completing the
exercise, my phone rang. It was my boyfriend. He asked where I had
been. I began to tell him that I had gone to see a counselor because
I was so devastated over what we had done. His reaction was swift
and harsh. He began yelling at me, calling me horrible names, and
said, "You promised you would never tell anyone!"

For the first time in six years, I saw clearly. It was as if the scales that
had me blinded had fallen off of my eyes, and I said without even
thinking, "You don't care about me. You care about you." I realized
everything had to do with him. It really wasn't all me. He had a
way of making me feel that I was always to blame for his anger and
controlling ways. I ended the relationship that day.

As I hung up the phone, a sense of peace came over me once
again, and I knew it was the right decision. I did not second-guess
myself. I felt a sense of power inside me where I had always felt
powerless. I never went back to him. He would call from time to

time. We have kept up with one another over the years. I forgave him, and I am sure he forgave me. I don't blame him for the big, ugly secret because I could have said no. I could have ended it long before he had the chance to hurt me over and over again. I am sure he is no longer the same person he was, and he has been kind through the years and now has a family of his own. We were two kids with big emotions, immature, and in need of wisdom and—most of all—Jesus.

I realized that, if I believed in the value God saw in me, I would never allow anyone to treat me badly again. I learned much from that relationship. There were so many good parts. If we are going to blame someone for all the bad parts of a relationship, we certainly need to blame them for all the good too! There were really good times and good things that happened. It was probably those good things that kept me around. I was exposed to higher-level leaders that expanded my thinking because of him. I graduated from college largely due to his encouragement and help. I learned that I could truly love someone more than I loved myself, what I loved in a relationship and what I loathed.

It wasn't all bad, and that's what's so tricky about trust.

It wasn't all bad, and that's what's so tricky about trust. There is usually good and bad all mixed in. We are getting something from that person that keeps us coming back. We must identify what is inside of us that allows us to settle for relationships that hurt us so deeply. If we are getting both positive and negative, then how much negative should we choose to endure? Is there an acceptable amount of negative? We might think things like, *After all, every couple argues. Isn't that normal?* Normal is subjective. That is a big issue. What is normal to one may be complete dysfunction to another. When we think normal, we think common. Just because abuse may be common doesn't mean it's right. It's the old parenting advice: "Just because everyone else is doing it doesn't mean you should. If they walked off a cliff, would you do it too?"

As I write this, the Gabby Petito case is fresh and painful to hear. Her fiancé was missing, and, later, his remains were found. Eyewitnesses allege he physically hit her and had a history of angry outbursts. There are so many questions surrounding the case. How long was abuse present? Did she confide in anyone? Why did she allow him to treat her that way? What did she believe about herself? Unfortunately, her case is representative of many others.

According to an NCBI Library article, ten million people every year are affected by family and domestic violence.[31] The ripple effects of abuse seem to be endless. The risk factors or reasons people abuse are many:

---

31 Martin R. Huecker, et al., "Domestic Violence," *NCBI Bookshelf*, 10 Feb. 2022, www.ncbi.nlm.nih.gov/books/NBK499891/.

- » Anger management issues
- » Jealousy,
- » Low self-esteem
- » Feeling inferior
- » Cultural beliefs that they have the right to control their partner
- » Personality disorder
- » Psychological disorders
- » Learned behavior from growing up in a family where domestic violence was accepted
- » Alcohol and drugs, as an impaired individual may be less likely to control violent impulses

There is never an excuse for abuse.

The best relationships I know are the ones built around God's principles. God's way of doing everything is simply the best way. God's way of doing relationships is so fulfilling. Our loving God has meticulously created us all in His image. Every person deserves to be honored simply because they are made in the image of God. I have talked to countless women who have stayed in physically and psychologically abusive marriages because their spouse convinced them that it was God's will, and they would be guilty of sin if they broke the marriage covenant. However, abuse and neglect violate the marriage covenant. It distorts the very image of God. Scripture condemns abuse and neglect in all its forms. It never gives a husband the right to dominate his wife.

In relationships, we are instructed to submit one to another. The husband is commanded to love his wife. Love is defined by God in 1 Corinthians 13:4-7 as patient, kind, not envious, not boastful, not proud, not rude, not selfish, not dishonoring, not easily angered. It keeps no record of wrongs, does not delight in doing evil, rejoices with the truth, always protects, always trusts, always hopes, and always perseveres. If your relationship doesn't look like God's definition of love, then it's not love. Many mistake lust for love, but the Word of God shows us that love gives and lust takes.

If your relationship doesn't look like God's
definition of love, then it's not love.

Chapter 11

RELATIONSHIP PHILOSOPHY

Timing, preparation, ability, strength, style, vulnerability, and risk are all essential in the art of dance and in the art of relationships. As we grow and learn, we want to live our lives with intentionality—by design and not default. To do this, we need to determine what our relationship philosophy is.

Here are a few questions to get you started as you define and write out your relationship philosophy.

- » What kind of a friend am I?
- » What kind of a friend do I want to be?
- » Repeat the above for each type of relationship you want to have.
- » What do I believe about the purpose of relationship?
- » What do I believe makes relationships healthy?
- » What are the best things about relationships?
- » What are the worst things about relationships?
- » How do I handle conflict?
- » How do I want those I am in relationship with to handle conflict?
- » What do I do when I am hurt?
- » What steps do I need to take to be the best version of me?
- » What steps do I need to take to be trustworthy?

You don't attract what you want; you attract what you are.

Once you write out your philosophy on relationships, create some "I am" or "I will" statements about how you will choose to operate. Once you've clearly defined this, you will grow toward it and attract like-minded people into your life. You don't attract what you want; you attract what you are. Focus on being the best version of yourself. It's the best gift that you can give to others. Below, you will find an excerpt of my philosophy. I know it will continue to grow as I do.

> *I believe every person is a gift. That God sends people into my life to bless me and that the enemy sends people in my life to curse me. It's up to me to discern the difference with the power of the Holy Spirit. Either way, I will choose to walk in love and forgiveness. I will do my best to love people the way they want to be loved. I am a great forgiver and apologizer. I will always move toward our relationship even when it's hard. I realize that, when someone expresses anger toward me, there is a need that they need me to meet. I will do my best to discover what the need is and meet it to the best of my ability. I will make it my responsibility to stop doing things that hurt my connection with others, and I will find out what strengthens our connection and do more of that.*

I choose to dwell with others with understanding. I will make it a point to listen to people who think differently than I do and seek to understand their point of view. I will keep my heart free from judgment. I fully embrace a growth mindset. I know what my core values are, and I build my life around them. I have firm boundaries to protect what I value most. I have an attitude of gratitude. I will believe the best about you even when the worst is displayed. My ego is not my amigo. I will choose to remember I don't deserve anything, and I am not above anything or anybody. I am blessed with all that I have been given, and I will remain thankful.

I treat others with honor not because they are honorable but because I am honorable. I am a powerful person who controls my emotions and takes responsibility for my actions. I am generous with my words and possessions. I will walk by faith and not by sight. I will think, speak, and act with love toward others. I will make it my highest goal to become the most loving person I can become. My words have power, and I will use them to build others up and bless them. I am a child of God before I am anything else, and I recognize my value comes from that alone. I recognize that others are made in His image, and I will treat them with honor.

I am a trustworthy person, and I will always trust the Lord.

MY STRENGTH

Yahweh is my strength and my wraparound shield. When I fully trust in you, help is on the way. I jump for joy and burst forth with ecstatic, passionate praise! I will sing songs of what you mean to me! You will be the inner strength of all your people, Yahweh, the mighty protector of all, and the saving strength for all your anointed ones. Save your people whom you love, and bless your chosen ones. Be our shepherd leading us forward, forever carrying us in your arms!

— Psalm 28:7-9 (TPT)

Epilogue

SAFE SPACE,
SAFE PEOPLE

I f you or I were ever asked to define what a safe space was, I'm quite sure we would all agree that it is a place where we would not be judged by anyone at any time. It would be a place where we could fully relax and be far removed from the challenges of life. However, the truth is that any place that involves having people in it will never be 100% safe, because people themselves are a challenge simply because we are imperfect. I think Proverbs 14:4 said it best: "The only clean stable is an empty stable."

It may be difficult for some people to believe, but church has always been my safe space. While I know there are many reading this today that are recovering from some form of church hurt, I personally can't remember ever having a bad experience at church until I became an adult. In fact, the phrase 'church hurt' has become so common today, you would believe it was happening in every church, but for me that wasn't the case. Which is why it hurts my heart whenever I see cases of abuse and immorality in the church. The stories of sexual misconduct, unethical financial practices, or domineering and manipulatilive leaders within the church can leave so many damaged. I ache for those who have experienced this, because it unfortunately did not have anything to do with the church as a whole, but rather with those who abused others through it. Every church that has hurt a person has also more than likely healed another, lumping every church together based on our own personal experiences rarely helps anyone.

When it comes to church hurt, we often just hear about the pain of those hurt by its pastors, but rarely do we hear about the pain that pastors may be enduring from something that a member has done, or perhaps one of their staff members. Pastors don't often publicize their pain or 'church hurt' for a few reasons:

First, they realize that it would do more damage than good to the body of Christ and they love and believe in the local church. Secondly, they trust God to fight their battles. When they know that an accusation is false, and that their character is being questioned and misrepresented, instead of defending themselves they choose to stay quiet and let God fight their battle. Everything in them wants to straighten out every outright lie, but they know it isn't best. People will choose to believe who they choose to believe with or without hearing their perspective, which is why most pastors rest in the great defender and their integrity.

Thirdly, they desire to stay true to scripture by trying to resolve issues in a biblical manner. The Word is clear that we are not to slander, gossip, or bring division. We are to go privately to the person and try to resolve it. If that doesn't work then we are to bring another person in to try to resolve it. When this process is followed it usually results in reconciliation because God's ways are best. The heart of God is always about reconciliation and connection. However this takes more than one willing party. Many people just walk away not realizing that they will bump into other issues wherever they go when they don't pursue reconciliation with those they have offended or have offended them.

I'll never forget how another pastor I know described full-time ministry. He called it 'brutiful' - in that it was both beautiful and brutal. After pastoring alongside my husband Michael for over 19 years, I would absolutely agree. It is the hardest thing I have ever done, because it involves being imperfect, while leading imperfect people. Throughout our ministry, we have been misunderstood, misjudged, betrayed, lied about, deeply wounded, stolen from, and slandered. We have shed many tears at the hands of people that we loved and trusted and thought that they loved us. We know that we are not alone, as many pastors have experienced the very same thing, but we rarely talk about it out of risk of revisiting the wound.

God hates when people sow discord inside His church. Sowing discord is when people say and do things that cause distrust with others. The 'sower' may act as though they are not attempting to cause arguments and fights but they are actively planting seeds of distrust, anger and even bitterness. It is often done in secret with whispers and side conversations. Sometimes with vague statements and innuendos on social media. They lack the conviction to talk to people with the goal of connection and resolution. They lack the courage and integrity to talk to you but have the audacity to talk about you. Their goal is never reconciliation, it's usually self elevation. They need a position, power or control in order for their ego to be satisfied. And in cases like these, a person's ego is never their amigo. They pretend to be ministering all the while they are only manipulating to get what they want.

The first time we ever experienced the pain of betrayal, it almost took me down. It hurt so badly. My filter and belief system was that if I just do the right things and love people well, no one will ever hurt me. How naive I was! When betrayal came knocking, I was never able to fully explain my perspective or straighten out any mis-understandings that this betrayal had caused. Every time I tried, it seemed as though things would get worse, because people seemed more interested in picking a side than wanting the truth. And worst of all, some people after picking a side would later choose to drop out and let go of their faith completely, which is in my opinion the greatest tragedy of any church hurt.

I'll never forget a story one of our pastor friends shared with us about when someone nearly split their church in two. This person wanted the pastor to extend to him more power and influence, and when it wasn't granted the way he wanted, he chose to leave the church and begin murmuring against it. He even went so far as to recruit others to leave with him, eventually beginning another church in the same town. Hearing this pastor share his pain over what had happened stuck with me for years. But what He chose to do in response was something I will never forget.

Instead of fighting his betrayer, he blessed him. After seeing member after member leave, including some leaders, this pastor decided to sow an offering into the new church! Where he probably had every natural right to sow bitterness and anger, he sowed love instead. This example of love has inspired my husband and I to ensure we always remain open when people come to us desiring to leave and join another church. Through the years, we have blessed and sent out a number of people who desired to start new ministries, or join others. However, there were others where it was extremely difficult to get behind, simply because their way of leaving was done in a deceitful way to cause hurt to others.

As a pastor, you lead your church often like you lead your home. You lead and feel things much like a parent would, so when something or someone hurts your children, you take it personally. When my son was bullied in middle school, I spent so many nights on my knees crying and praying that I could ever forgive those who hurt my son. The same is true when it comes to those I pastor. When our members are bullied with lies, or something comes to attack the character of our 'spiritual' house, I take it personally.

Although learning to be quiet has been a great strategy against the enemy, I can also remember situations where we did not address issues earlier on that we saw coming. The minute we sensed discord, complaining or murmuring, we should have swiftly dealt with it, instead of thinking it would just go away. Discord never just goes away, it only grows under the surface and emerges in more places than any one person can correct. The enemy is just that crafty. He loves nothing more than to further divide God's people and have us tear each other down, and as a result, tear His church down.

I have learned that healthy Pastors love people, even people who hurt you. And while we would love to reconcile with everyone who has hurt or left us, one of the best gifts we can ever give people is the gift of goodbye. Sometimes the best thing we can do is to let people go, even when they refuse to acknowledge what they did and how they hurt us. When people walk away from you, let them walk. Our relationships, even inside the church, can be for a reason, season and for some, a lifetime. So we have to learn how to do the difficult job of placing a boundary to protect our hearts, and in this era of social media, where passive aggressive innuendos and statements are as prevalent as ever between people, these boundaries are so important for us as believers.

While I am not a fan of cancel culture, moving past church hurt as a pastor has required me to block some people on social media just to protect my heart and my eyes. I have found that doing so has helped to keep my heart soft and my eyes on the mission and the great prize which is the Lord Jesus Christ. Because our battles are not with flesh and blood (even when it feels like it sometimes), our enemy is not the person who hurt us, but the one who has used people to hurt us. One of my favorite scriptures is Luke 7:47, "her sins, which are many, are forgiven—for she loved much. He who is forgiven little, loves little." What an amazing reminder and challenge to all of us, especially to those of who are pastors! Because I have been forgiven of so much by God, how can I withhold forgiveness from someone else?

Overcoming evil with good is how we become trustworthy. And our churches will become the trustworthy, safe spaces that people need when we learn to live out our days with the love of God.

"Love does not traffic in shame and disrespect, nor selfishly seek its own honor. Love is not easily irritated or quick to take offense. Love joyfully celebrates honesty and finds no delight in what is wrong. Love is a safe place of shelter, for it never stops believing the best for others."- 1 Corinthians

> *"Some want to live within the sound*
> *Of church or chapel bell;*
> *I want to run a rescue shop,*
> *Within a yard of hell."*
> —C.T. Studd

Knowledge is what to do. Wisdom is how to do it.

May you grow in both wisdom and knowledge as you become Trustworthy,

Xoxo,
—Charla

This is me at a formal dance
smiling on the outside but
hurting deeply on the inside.

My friend Dana is with me at our
favorite summer spot, my backyard
pool. She is leaning on me, but it
was me that needed to lean on
her a few years later. She took
me to the counselor and was a
steady source of encouragement.

College sorority composite
photo taken before the event
that would mark a major
Turning Point in my life.

Kris Ramsahai
Atlanta International Fellowship
The loving Missionary that
my friend Dana took me
to see for Counseling.

My incredible parents, celebrating my college
graduation at UGA between the hedges.

The family I didn't deserve but God graciously blessed me with.
Pictured (left to right) Micha (Michael Jr.),
Charla, Michael, Madelyn, and Presley.

The most recent picture of our family. I'm holding on
tight these days. They are growing into adults and the
page is turning as we enter the next chapter!

$\wedge$V$\wedge$IL +

TRY FOR 30 DAYS *AND RECEIVE*
THE SEQUENCE TO SUCCESS
BUNDLE FREE

$79 VALUE

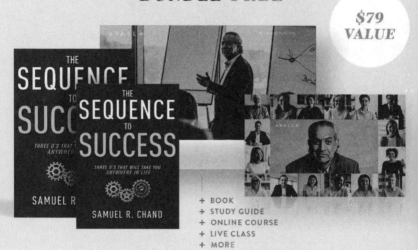

+ BOOK
+ STUDY GUIDE
+ ONLINE COURSE
+ LIVE CLASS
+ MORE

The Art *of* Leadership

This isn't just another leadership collective...this is the next level of networking, resources, and empowerment designed specifically for leaders like you.

Whether you're an innovator in ministry, business, or your community, **AVAIL +** is designed to take you to your next level. Each one of us needs connection. Each one of us needs practical advice. Each one of us needs inspiration. **AVAIL +** is all about equipping you, so that you can turn around and equip those you lead.

THEARTOFLEADERSHIP.COM/CHAND